EXPLORING SCIENCE 7

INTERNATIONAL 11-14

Mark Levesley, Sue Kearsey, Ian Bradley, Alice Jenson, Sarah Longshaw, Penny Johnson

WORKBOOK

T0346311

P Pearson

CONTENTS

1 Doctors use tests to see if there are changes in a person's body compared to normal. List three tests a doctor may perform.

i ....

ii ....

iii ....

B

2 A doctor tells a patient that they have acne. Suggest what evidence the doctor has found to make them think this.

....

3 What does 'evidence' mean? Tick (✔) *one* box.
- ☐ **A** the name given to a certain type of disease
- ☐ **B** changes in the way that the body works
- ☐ **C** information used to say whether something is right or wrong
- ☐ **D** a type of test performed by a doctor

B

4a Which of the following best describes the heart? Tick (✔) *one* box.
- ☐ **A** an organ
- ☐ **B** a cell
- ☐ **C** a tissue
- ☐ **D** a system

b State one job that the heart does. ....

5 In groups, discuss how to tell if something is alive. Record your group's ideas in the first box below. Ignore the other box for the moment! There is no right or wrong answer.

Ideas from my group:

....

....

....

What we now think:

....

....

7Aa LIFE PROCESSES

1 Tick (✓) the living organisms in this list.
   ☐ elephant   ☐ soccer ball   ☐ robot   ☐ pine tree
   ☐ aeroplane   ☐ human   ☐ desert   ☐ mouse

2 A mnemonic (pronounced 'nem-**on**-ic') is a word or phrase that helps you to remember a list.
   MRS GREN is a mnemonic to remember the life processes.

a What is a life process? ....

   ....

b Draw *one* line from each letter to a life process. Then draw *one* line from each life process to its meaning.
   One has been done for you.

   Life process   **Meaning**

   M   nutrition   increasing in size

   R   respiration   getting rid of waste

   S   reproduction ───── making new life

   G   growth   releasing energy

   R   movement   changing position

   E   sensitivity   detecting changes in the surroundings

   N   excretion   needing substances to carry on living

3 What do humans need to respire? Tick (✓) *two* boxes.
   ☐ oxygen   ☐ carbon dioxide   ☐ wood
   ☐ fire   ☐ food   ☐ light

4 Describe one way in which the growth of trees is different from the growth of humans.

   ....

SB 5a In what ways is a car like an organism? ....

   ....

b Why is a car not an organism? ....

   ....

6 In your group, look at your answers to question **5** on page 3. Discuss your ideas again to find out if they
   have changed. If you can, write a better answer in the lower box.

7Ab ORGANS

1 Use a *pencil* to tick (✓) *one* box to answer to each question.

a Which organ lets you think?
- ☐ **A** heart
- ☐ **B** brain
- ☐ **C** skull
- ☐ **D** liver

b Which organ pumps blood?
- ☐ **A** heart
- ☐ **B** kidney
- ☐ **C** lungs
- ☐ **D** liver

c A job of the stomach is to:
- ☐ **A** store waste materials.
- ☐ **B** make urine.
- ☐ **C** break up food.
- ☐ **D** help you breathe.

d A job of the liver is to:
- ☐ **A** destroy some substances.
- ☐ **B** absorb food.
- ☐ **C** make urine.
- ☐ **D** excrete water.

e A sheep's lungs excrete:
- ☐ **A** mucus.
- ☐ **B** carbon dioxide.
- ☐ **C** urine.
- ☐ **D** oxygen.

f The tube taking food to the stomach is the:
- ☐ **A** intestine.
- ☐ **B** diaphragm.
- ☐ **C** oesophagus.
- ☐ **D** trachea.

2 Ask your teacher how many of your answers to question **1** are correct. Then work with others and the Student Book to find your incorrect answers. Make corrections and check with your teacher. Do this until they are all correct.

3 Give the name of the organ that humans use for sensitivity. ....

4 Give the name of the organ that plants use for nutrition. ....

5 State two functions of a plant root.

i ....

ii ....

6a What process produces the food stored in plant storage organs?

....

b Why won't a potato grow if the potato plant does not get much light?

....

....

....

1 Complete the sentences using words from the box. Use each word once.

| conclusion | diagnosis | doctors | evidence | explain | test |

Scientists invent ideas to try to _____ things that they see happening. They

then do experiments to _____ their ideas. They use the results from their tests

as _____, to decide if an idea is correct or incorrect. This decision is called a

_____. Medical _____ also use this process to try

to work out what is wrong with someone. A conclusion about what is wrong with someone is called a

_____.

2 Look at the drawing.

a What organ is the doctor examining?

_____

b What is the function of this organ?

_____

_____

3 Draw *one* line from each symptom to the organ that is the cause.

Evidence (or 'symptom')

only small amount of urine produced

difficulty breathing

very fast pulse

sore chest after eating food

Diagnosis

stomach problem

kidney problem

lung problem

heart problem

SB **4** You can use these items to make different stethoscopes.

a Describe how to test a stethoscope. _____

_____

b Explain how to judge which design of stethoscope is best. _____

_____

1 Complete the sentences using words from the box.
Use each word more than once.

| organ | tissue |

Every .... in your body is made of many different

types of .... An example of a .... is fat.

An example of an important .... in your body is your liver.

2 The diagram shows a slice through a plant root.

a What is the function of root hair tissue?

....

root hair tissue

b On the diagram, write in the name of the central
tissue (which carries water in a plant).

c How many tissues in total are found in this root?

....

3 Explain how you can identify one of the tissues
in your tongue. To answer this, tick (✔) *one* box
for each of parts **a** and **b** below.

a A tissue in your tongue is:
- ☐ **A** hair.
- ☐ **B** root hair tissue.
- ☐ **C** bone.
- ☐ **D** muscle.

b You know this because:
- ☐ **A** your tongue is hard.
- ☐ **B** your tongue feels furry.
- ☐ **C** you can move your tongue.
- ☐ **D** your tongue is wet.

4 The leaf of a plant is an organ.

a Give a function of a leaf. ....

b Suggest one tissue that it contains. ....

c Explain why you think it contains this tissue. ....

....

5 Complete the table.

Organ	Example of tissue	Function of tissue
heart		

6 What sort of organ is a carrot? ....

1 Describe what a microscope is used for.

....

....

....

2 Complete the labels on the microscope, to show the names of the parts.

3a Number these sentences in order, to describe how to use a microscope.

[ ] Look down a microscope with both eyes open and adjust the light source.

[ ] Make the gap between the stage and the lens as small as possible.

[ ] Place a slide on the stage. Use the clips to hold the slide in place.

[ ] Move the lowest power lens over the hole in the stage.

[ ] To magnify more, use the next most powerful lens. Use the fine focusing wheel to adjust the focus.

[ ] Widen the gap between the stage and the lens, until what you see is clear (in focus).

light source

fine focusing wheel

b Describe how you would 'widen the gap', between the stage and the lens.

....

....

SB

4 What is a specimen?

5a Write instructions for these diagrams to describe how to make a slide.

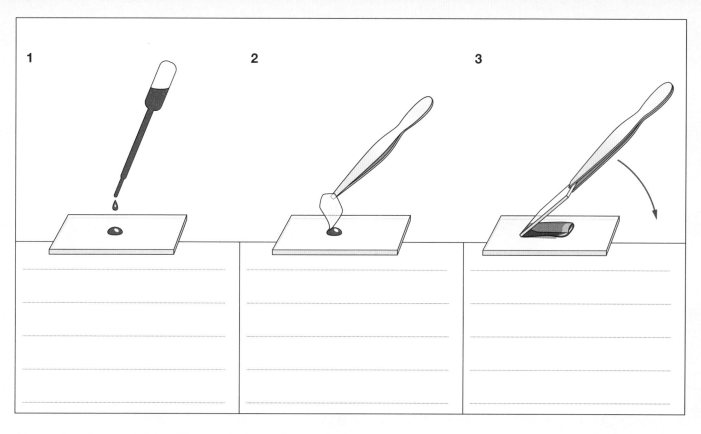

1

2

3

b Share your instructions with others. Discuss which instructions are best and why. On the lines below, write an improved version of *one* of your instructions.

....

....

c How have you improved this instruction? ....

....

6 Why do we use coverslips? ....

....

7 Complete the table.

Eyepiece lens power	Objective lens power	Total magnification
×5	×10	
×7.5	×15	
	×20	×200

1 The diagram shows an animal cell. Label the parts.

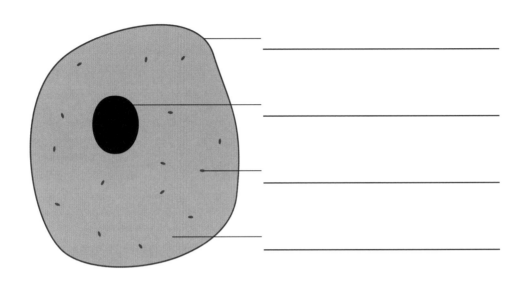

2 Draw *one* line from each plant cell part to its function.

Cell part

chloroplast

large vacuole

nucleus

cell wall

Function

controls the cell

rigid box that helps support the cell

storage space

where photosynthesis occurs

3 Explain why root cells do not have a part that leaf cells have.
To answer this, tick (✓) *one* box for each of parts **a** and **b** below.

a Root cells do not have:
- ☐ **A** chloroplasts.
- ☐ **B** mitochondria.
- ☐ **C** a vacuole.
- ☐ **D** cell walls.

b This is because:
- ☐ **A** the roots need to be flexible.
- ☐ **B** there is no light underground.
- ☐ **C** root cells do not respire.
- ☐ **D** roots do not store substances.

4 A cell is magnified ×600. What does this mean? Tick (✓) *one* box.
- ☐ **A** It looks 600 times smaller than its real size.
- ☐ **B** There are now 600 cells instead of one cell.
- ☐ **C** It looks 600 times bigger than its real size.
- ☐ **D** Only one cell out of 600 is shown.

5 What makes some plant cells green? ....

6 In what part of a cell would you find cellulose? ....

7 Complete the Venn diagram using the names of cell parts.

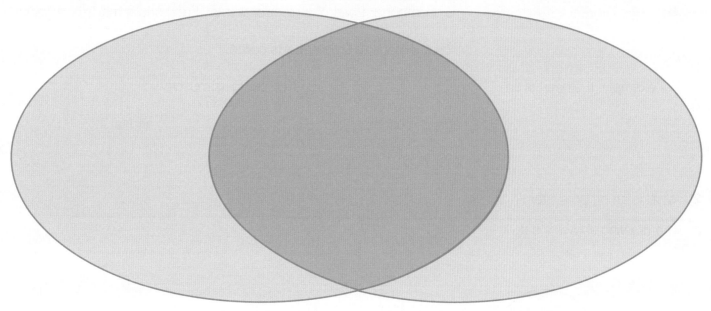

only in animal cells   **in both animal and plant cells**   **only in plant cells**

8 A leaf cell from a *Eucalyptus* tree is 0.012 mm wide. Calculate its width at a magnification of ×5000.

....

9a Discuss with others in your group how to draw a labelled diagram of a root hair cell. What parts would you include? How would you do your drawing?

b Draw and label a root hair cell in the space below.

1   Complete the sentences using words from the box. You may use some words more than once.

cell	cells	tissue	tissues	organ	organs

The basic 'building blocks' of all organisms are _____. A group of these

'building blocks' of the same type and working together is called a _____.

An _____ is an important part of a plant or animal. Each one is made of different

_____, which are made of smaller parts called _____.

For example, the heart is an _____ that contains muscle

_____ (made of muscle _____) and fat

_____ (made of fat _____).

SB   2   What is an organ system? _____

3   The drawing shows a cat.

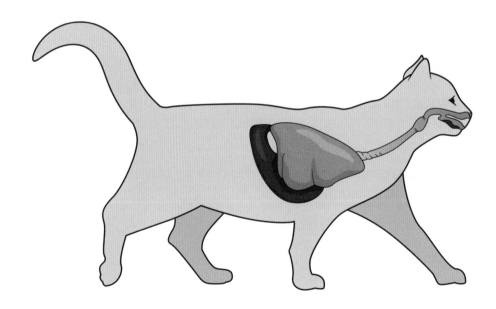

a   What organ system is shown? _____

b   On the drawing, label *two* parts of this organ system.

4 The drawing shows a chicken.

a What organ system is shown?

....

b On the drawing, label *two* parts of this organ system.

c What is the function of this organ system?

....

....

....

5a Draw *one* line from each life process to an organ system that helps with this.

b Draw *two* lines from each organ system to show two organs it contains.

Life process	Organ system	Organs
excretion	breathing system	bladder
		bone
movement	locomotor system	brain
		kidney
respiration	nervous system	lung
		muscle
sensitivity	urinary system	spinal cord
		trachea

6a What are the organs in a plant's water transport system? ....

b Name one tissue you would expect to find in all these organs. ....

7 Explain one thing that plants need a constant supply of. To answer this, tick (✓) *one* box for each of parts **a** and **b** below.

a Plants need a constant supply of:
- ☐ **A** light.
- ☐ **B** water.
- ☐ **C** wind.
- ☐ **D** sugar.

b This is because:
- ☐ **A** they lose it by photosynthesis.
- ☐ **B** they lose it during digestion.
- ☐ **C** they lose it by reflection.
- ☐ **D** they lose it by evaporation.

7Ae TRANSPLANTS

1a Describe what is meant by the term organ transplant. ....

....

b Suggest one effect on someone's body if their heart is not working properly.

....

2a In the space below, draw a diagram to show how organ systems, organs, tissues and cells are linked. In your diagram, use one example from plants and one from humans.

b Share your diagram with others. Discuss whether the diagrams in your group:
- are correct
- show enough information
- are easy to understand.

c Write down two ways in which your diagram is good.

i ....

ii ....

d Write down one thing that you could improve about your diagram.

....

3 The table shows a 'confidence grid'. Tick (✓) *one* box for each statement in the table.

Statement	Definitely correct	Might be correct	Might be wrong	Definitely wrong
a Chloroplasts can be found in plant cells but not animal cells.				
b Mitochondria can be found in animal cells but not plant cells.				
c A cell surface membrane controls what enters and leaves a cell.				
d A group of cells of the same type form an organ.				

1 Suggest two reasons why rare animals are kept in zoos.

i ....

ii ....

2 Why do you think there are not large numbers of Canadian lynx in Devon, even though one escaped?

....

....

3 In a group, discuss the four types of evidence below. Decide which best supports the idea that there are wild wallabies living on the Isle of Man. Put a tick (✓) next to your choice, and then give a reason for your choice.

- ☐ **A** photograph showing a wallaby close-up with little background
- ☐ **B** photograph showing a wallaby with background that is clearly Isle of Man
- ☐ **C** description from someone who says they saw a wallaby on the Isle of Man
- ☐ **D** drawing of a wallaby from someone who is on the Isle of Man

The best evidence is ....

Our reason for choosing this is ....

....

4 Wallabies and cats are both mammals. Suggest two ways in which you would expect their reproduction to be similar.

i ....

ii ....

5 Ovaries are part of the female reproductive system. They contain different types of cells, including egg cells. Tick (✓) the box that best describes an ovary.

- ☐ **A** organ system
- ☐ **B** organ
- ☐ **C** tissue
- ☐ **D** cell

1 Draw *one* line from each stage of the scientific method to its definition.

Stage

observation

hypothesis

prediction

data

Definition

information collected from an experiment

what will happen if a hypothesis is correct

something that was seen (can lead to a question)

an idea that could answer a question

2 The diagram shows one way to do the scientific method. Complete each blank box in the diagram using a word from the box. Use some words more than once.

data   hypothesis   prediction

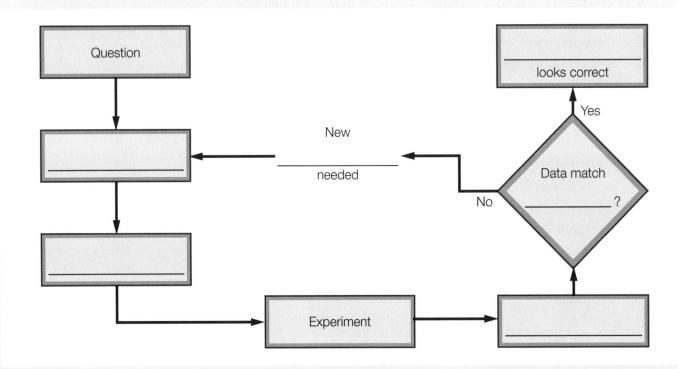

SB

3 Tick (✓) one box in each row to show whether each statement is a hypothesis, a prediction or a result.

Statement	Hypothesis	Prediction	Result
The seeds at the warmer temperature sprouted first.	☐	☐	☐
The ability of animals to reproduce depends on there being males and females.	☐	☐	☐
If people lack vitamin C in their food, then they will get a disease called scurvy.	☐	☐	☐

4 Read the method for an experiment to test the hypothesis that rotten banana peel produces flies.

Method

A | Peel a ripe banana and place half of the peel in each of two jars.

B | Immediately place gauze over the top of one jar and secure it with an elastic band.

C | Stand the jars outside. (You should see small flies entering the jar with no gauze.)

D | After a few hours, make sure there are no flies in the open jar, then cover it with gauze as you did for the first jar.

E | Bring both jars inside and observe for 2 weeks.

a Give a reason why the two jars are set up differently.

....

....

b If the hypothesis that rotten banana peel produces flies is correct, predict the results.

Predicted result in jar covered after a few hours ....

Predicted result in jar covered from the start ....

5 This description is a 300-year-old recipe for mice.

**Place some sweaty clothes in a jar with some wheat. Wait for 21 days.
The sweat will turn the wheat into mice.**

Discuss the recipe in a small group and write a question, a hypothesis and a prediction for an experiment to test the recipe.

Question: ....

....

Hypothesis: ....

....

Prediction: ....

....

1 Use words from the box to answer the questions. You may use each word more than once.

egg cell	gamete	sperm cell	zygote

a A scientific word that means a sex cell. ....

b The meaning of the word ovum. ....

c A male sex cell of an animal. ....

d A female sex cell of an animal. ....

e A scientific word that means a fertilised egg cell. ....

2a Write a passage with some missing words to describe what happens during fertilisation. The words to miss out are in the box. Then ask a friend to complete your text.

egg	fertilisation	fuse	nuclei	sperm	zygote

....

....

....

b Check what your friend has done. Then discuss the good points of the exercise and what improvements could be made. Write one improvement on the line below.

....

SB

3a Name an animal that uses internal fertilisation. ....

b Give two reasons why the females of this animal produce only a few egg cells.

i ....

ii ....

SB

4 A female mouthbrooder fish sucks her fertilised eggs into her mouth, where they hatch. Complete the sentence to explain whether you would expect mouthbrooder females to produce more or fewer egg cells than other fish of the same size.

I would expect mouthbrooder females to produce .... eggs

because ....

7Bb REPRODUCTIVE ORGANS

1 Label the diagram of the male reproductive system.

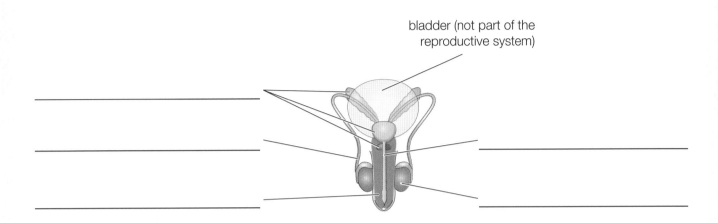

bladder (not part of the reproductive system)

2 Draw *one* line from each part of the male reproductive system to its function.

Part	Function
testis	carries sperm to the penis
gland	carries semen to outside the body
sperm duct	produces sperm
urethra	produces fluids that provide energy for sperm

3a Tick (✓) *one* box to show if you think sperm cells need to be warmer, cooler or the same temperature as the body to develop.

☐ warmer   ☐ cooler   ☐ same temperature

b Explain your reasoning.

4 Describe one adaptation of a sperm cell that helps it enter an egg cell.

5 Explain two ways in which a sperm cell is adapted for swimming.

i

ii

6 Complete the following sentences using words from the box.

cervix	ovary	oviduct	uterus	vagina

In females, an egg cell is released from an _____ every month (from

puberty until menopause). The egg cell passes along an _____ till it reaches

the _____ . At the bottom of the uterus is a muscular ring called the

_____. This ring connects the uterus to the _____,

which leads to the outside.

7 Write the function of each structure beside its label on the diagram on the right.

8 A zygote (fertilised egg cell) needs a supply of energy for cell division and growth of the early embryo. Explain how the zygote has a supply of energy.

_____

_____

_____

_____

jelly coat	cell surface membrane

9a Who produces gametes for the longest period of their life? Tick (✓) one box.

☐ **A** men
☐ **B** same for men and women
☐ **C** women
☐ **D** neither sex produces gametes

b Why do you think your answer to part **a** is correct? Tick (✓) one box.

☐ **A** men go through menopause
☐ **B** women go through menopause
☐ **C** neither men nor women go through menopause
☐ **D** both men and women go through menopause

cytoplasm	nucleus

7BC BECOMING PREGNANT

1 Draw *one* line from each scientific term to its definition.

Scientific term		Definition
implantation		when male and female gamete nuclei fuse
pregnancy		when semen leaves the erect penis
fertilisation		when an embryo sinks into the uterus lining
ejaculation		when a baby develops from a zygote in a woman's uterus

2 Where does fertilisation occur?

....

3 Complete the following sentences using words from the box.

umbilical cord	amniotic fluid	placenta

A bag containing .... develops around an embryo. The embryo also

develops an organ called the .... within the uterus lining. This organ

connects to the embryo by the ....

4a Write down the function of each of the following.

placenta: ....

amnion: ....

umbilical cord: ....

b With a partner, compare what you have written for each function. Look for ways to improve your answers to part **a**. Write your improved answers below.

placenta: ....

amnion: ....

umbilical cord: ....

7Bd GESTATION AND BIRTH

1 Write a number in each box to show how long each stage is in humans.

embryo: ☐ weeks   foetus: ☐ weeks   gestation: ☐ months

SB

2a Suggest two advantages of having ultrasound scans during pregnancy. Give a reason for each advantage.

Advantage 1: ....

Reason 1: ....

Advantage 2: ....

Reason 2: ....

b Compare your answers with a partner and decide on *one* answer in part **a** that you could improve. Write your better answer below.

....

....

3 Number the stages of labour in the order in which they happen.
The first one has been done for you.

☐ 1   The muscles in the uterus wall start to contract.

☐   The uterus muscles contract strongly to push out the afterbirth (placenta).

☐   The uterus muscles contract very strongly and push the baby out through the vagina.

☐   The cervix muscles relax, making the cervix wider.

4a Explain why vaccinating a girl against rubella can help protect against harm to her foetus when she is a woman.

....

....

b Give *one* advantage of feeding a newborn baby on breast milk.

....

....

1 State the reason why Arabian oryx became extinct in the wild.

2a Use this table to list similarities and differences between conditions in the red panda's habitat and in a zoo in your country.

Condition	Natural habitat	Zoo

b Use your table to decide what your enclosure needs. Draw your design below and label it to show the key design points. Be prepared to present your design to the class, explaining your reasons for the main parts of the design.

7Be GROWING UP

1 Tick (✓) the box that shows the age at which puberty usually starts.

☐ **A** birth

☐ **B** 10–15 years

☐ **C** 30–35 years

☐ **D** about 50 years

2 The table shows changes that happen in humans during puberty.

stronger body smell		testes start to make sperm cells	
hair grows on face and chest		hair grows in armpits	
voice deepens (or 'breaks')		hips get wider	
ovaries start to release egg cells		testes and penis get bigger	
pubic hair grows		shoulders grow wider	

a Write B in the box beside any changes that happen in boys' bodies.

b Write G in the box beside any changes that happen in girls' bodies.

c Circle the changes that must happen before a boy or girl can reproduce.

3 Compare your answers to question **2** with a partner to identify any incorrect answers. Write any corrections in a different colour on the table.

4 Complete the following sentences using words from the box.

adolescence	acne	emotional	ovaries	sex hormones	testes

During puberty, more _____ are released in the body. In boys, these

substances are produced by the _____. In girls, these substances are

produced by the _____ and brain.

These substances cause physical changes and can also cause _____. Apart

from physical changes, they also cause _____ changes, which are a natural

part of _____.

5 State what happens during ovulation.

_____

_____

6 The diagram shows the menstrual cycle.

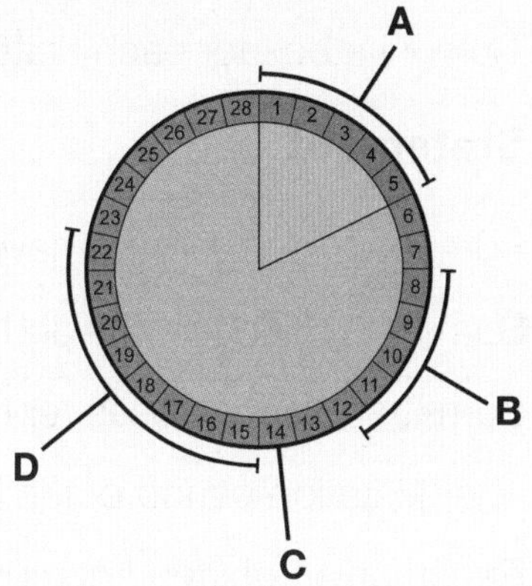

a Which letter shows when ovulation happens? Tick ✓ one box.

☐ **A**   ☐ **B**   ☐ **C**   ☐ **D**

b Which letter shows when menstruation happens? Tick ✓ one box.

☐ **A**   ☐ **B**   ☐ **C**   ☐ **D**

c Describe what is happening in the uterus during stage D shown in the cycle.

_____

_____

d Explain why the change that happens at D is important if the woman becomes pregnant.

_____

7 Look at the cycle in the diagram in question **6**.

a Name the first stage that will *not* happen if the egg cell is fertilised.

_____

b Use your answer to part **a** to say how a woman might tell if she is pregnant.

_____

8 You are going to draw a diagram of the human life cycle in the space below.

a On a separate piece of paper, write down the words you want to include.

b Share your ideas with a partner or group. Discuss why you have chosen these words and where they would go.

c Finalise your ideas and draw your diagram in the space below.

1 Panamanian golden frogs and Sumatran rhinoceroses are being bred in zoos.

a Tick (✓) a box for each statement below to show if it is true or false.

Statement	True	False
i Sumatran rhinoceroses have a longer gestation period than Panamanian golden frogs.	☐	☐
ii Sumatran rhinoceroses and Panamanian golden frogs are both endangered.	☐	☐
iii Sumatran rhinoceroses reproduce by internal fertilisation.	☐	☐
iv The gestation period of the Sumatran rhinoceros is the same length as in humans.	☐	☐
v Panamanian golden frogs produce fewer offspring than Sumatran rhinoceroses in the same time.	☐	☐
vi A female Sumatran rhinoceros can be made pregnant by inserting sperm into her oviducts.	☐	☐

b Compare your answers with a partner to check for mistakes. Mark any corrections to your list in a different colour.

2 The natural habitat of Panamanian golden frogs is next to fast-flowing streams on the mountain slopes of Panama in Central America.

Describe how a zoo could provide the best conditions in an enclosure for breeding Panamanian golden frogs. Use a labelled drawing to help you.

....

....

....

1a Tick (✓) the correct box to show the organ system that each organ belongs to.

Organ	Circulatory system	Digestive system	Excretory system	Gas exchange system
heart	☐	☐	☐	☐
small intestine	☐	☐	☐	☐
bladder	☐	☐	☐	☐
stomach	☐	☐	☐	☐
diaphragm	☐	☐	☐	☐
kidneys	☐	☐	☐	☐
lungs	☐	☐	☐	☐
oesophagus (gullet)	☐	☐	☐	☐
large intestine	☐	☐	☐	☐

b Check your answers with a partner. Mark any corrections on the table in a different colour.

2 The diagram shows a section through a blood vessel.

a Is a blood vessel an organ system, an organ or a tissue?

....

b Give a reason for your answer.

....

....

inner surface covered in a thin layer of epithelial cells

thick wall made of layers, including a layer of elastic fibres and a layer of muscle cells

3 In a group, discuss ways of judging fitness for each of the S-factors. Write down the best idea for each factor below.

suppleness ....

strength ....

speed ....

stamina ....

1 Draw *one* line from each scientific term to its definition.

Scientific term	Definition
ventilation	when waste substances leave the body
gas exchange	the cell process that releases energy and produces carbon dioxide
respiration	when oxygen enters blood in the lungs and carbon dioxide leaves the blood
excretion	when air moves into and out of the lungs

SB

2 Describe how gases are carried around your body.

....

....

....

3 Sheep, cats and humans are all mammals.

a This list shows some organs of a sheep: trachea, diaphragm, lungs.

Name the organ system that these organs belong to. ....

b Name *two* organs of the circulatory system in cats.

....

4 Describe how the muscle cells in tissue between the ribs are adapted to allow breathing.

....

....

5 Explain what happens during inhalation. To answer this, tick (✔) *one* box in each of parts **a** and **b** below.

a In inhalation:
- ☐ **A** air enters the lungs.
- ☐ **B** air leaves the lungs.
- ☐ **C** air circulates inside the lungs.
- ☐ **D** air leaves the blood.

b This happens because:
- ☐ **A** muscles between the ribs relax, so the ribs move down and in.
- ☐ **B** muscles in the diaphragm contract, so the diaphragm moves downwards.
- ☐ **C** muscles in the trachea contract to suck air into the lungs.
- ☐ **D** muscles in the nose cause it to open and suck air into the lungs.

7Cb MUSCLES AND BLOOD

1 The diagram shows part of the circulatory system of a goat.

a Complete the labels in the diagram using words from the box.

> artery   capillaries
>
> lungs   muscle   vein

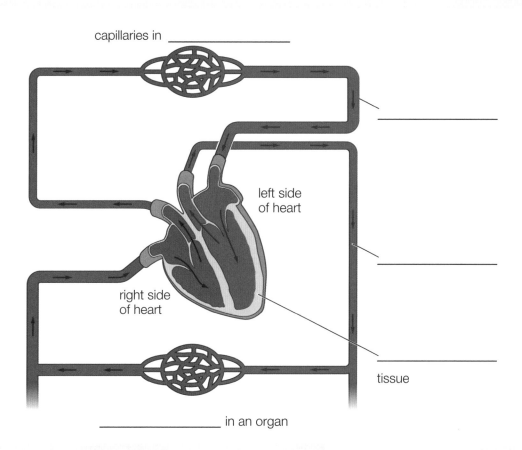

capillaries in _____

left side
of heart

right side
of heart

tissue

_____ in an organ

b Does a goat have a single or double circulatory system? ....

c Give a reason for your answer to part **b**.

....

d Describe the function of the tissue labelled on the heart.

....

e Look carefully at the diagram above. Suggest why the left-hand side of the heart has more of this tissue.

....

....

2 Tick (✓) *one* box to show where blood cells are made.

☐ in the heart   ☐ in the brain

☐ in bone marrow   ☐ in blood vessels

3 Complete the sentences about blood using words from the box.

| plasma | red blood cells | white blood cells |

a Nutrients and waste are carried in blood dissolved in ....

b Oxygen is carried by haemoglobin found in ....

c .... help to fight infections.

d .... have a special disc shape with a large surface area.

4 The table shows the blood pressure and rate of blood flow through three different types of blood vessel.

a Which blood vessel carries blood at the highest pressure?

Vessel	Blood pressure (kPa)	Rate of blood flow (cm/s)
artery	10.5	35.0
capillary	1.6	<0.1
vein	1.3	5.0

The diagram shows sections through the blood vessels.

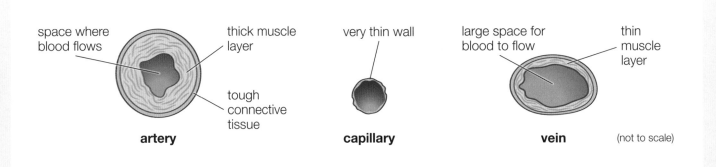

b Look at the diagram. Describe how the blood vessel you named in part **a** is adapted to carrying blood at the highest pressure.

....

SB

c Describe how capillaries are adapted for the exchange of substances between blood and tissues.

....

d Suggest one adaptation of veins for allowing blood to flow easily at the pressure shown in the table.

....

1a Tick (✓) the correct box to show whether each question is a scientific, non-scientific and/or an ethical question.

Question	Scientific	Non-scientific but not ethical	Non-scientific and ethical
i Are parts of a taxi driver's brain bigger than average?	☐	☐	☐
ii Should William Harvey have killed animals to use for his experiments?	☐	☐	☐
iii Do older people generally have lower pulse rates than younger people?	☐	☐	☐
iv Do roses smell nicer than freesia flowers?	☐	☐	☐
v Does exercise affect your pulse rate?	☐	☐	☐

b Compare your answers with a partner to check for any mistakes. Mark any corrections in a different colour.

2a Give a reason why you marked a particular question in question **1a** as being ethical.

....

b Describe the difference between a scientific question and a non-scientific question.

....

....

c Work with a partner to come up with three more questions for **1a** – one of each type.

scientific ....

non-scientific but not ethical ....

non-scientific and ethical ....

3 Choose one of the scientific questions in question **1a** and suggest what information could be gathered from investigations to find the answer.

....

....

SB **1** Draw *one* line from each part of the skeleton to its main function.

Part

knee joint

backbone

skull

Function

support

protection

movement

2 Look at the diagram of the skull.

Explain how the joints of the skull help the skull be adapted to its function.

....

....

....

....

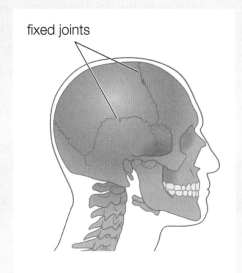

fixed joints

3a Give a reason why bones need to be strong.

....

b Give a reason why bones need to be light.

....

SB **c** Explain why a large bone can be both strong and light.

....

....

4 How confident are you at identifying the positions and functions of these parts of the skeleton? Complete the faces in the boxes to show your confidence – the bigger the smile, the more confident you are.

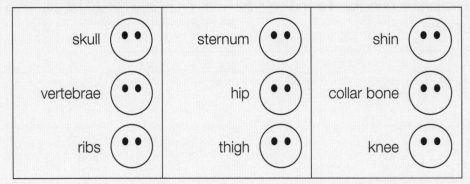

5a Label the diagram of an elbow joint using words from the box.

| bone | cartilage | ligament |
| muscle | tendon | |

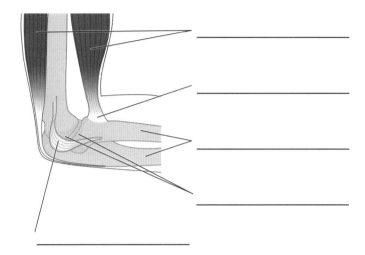

_____

_____

_____

_____

_____

b What causes bones to move? ....

c Complete the sentences about tissues of the skeleton by writing one word in each space.

Cartilage tissue is ...., which helps the ends of bones in a joint slide past

each other. Tendons attach .... to bones, so that bones in a joint can move.

Ligaments hold the .... in a joint together to prevent dislocation.

6 The diagram shows the possible movement in two kinds of flexible joint.

Which type of flexible joint is found in the elbow?

Give a reason for your answer.

....

....

....

hinge joint

allows bending in only one direction

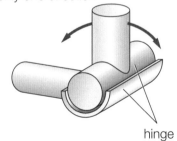

hinge

ball and socket joint

allows twisting and bending

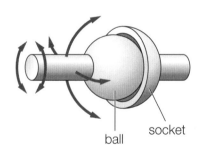

ball   socket

b Which of these joints allows movement in the most directions? ....

c Name *two* 'ball and socket' joints in the human body.

1 Name *two* organs in the locomotor system.

....

2 Hasim starts training for a race by running 10 km every day.

a In which part of his body will the muscles change most due to his training?

....

b Complete the sentence to explain how the force generated by those muscles changes due to training.

The force generated by the muscles will ....

because the muscles ....

c Suggest how the bones to which those muscles attach will change as a result of Hasim's training. Give a reason for your answer.

....

....

3 Tick (✓) any correct statement(s).
- ☐ **A** When muscles contract they can pull on bones.
- ☐ **B** When muscles contract they can push on bones.
- ☐ **C** When muscles relax they can pull on bones.
- ☐ **D** When muscles relax they can push on bones.
- ☐ **E** When muscles relax they cannot push or pull on bones.

4 Nina decides to pick up a pencil. Describe how Nina's brain controls the muscles in her hand so she can do that.

....

....

....

....

5 Give a reason why muscle cells contain many mitochondria.

....

6 The diagram shows two muscles that move the lower arm.

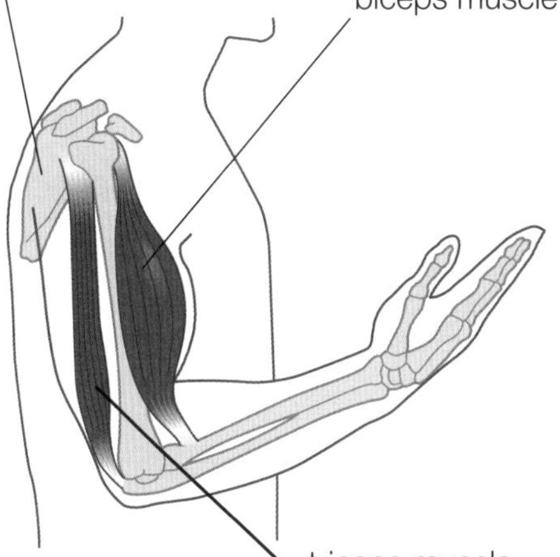

a Use the diagram to help you complete these sentences.

When the biceps muscle contracts it ....

one of the lower arm bones so the lower arm

.... This movement stretches the relaxed

triceps muscle. When the triceps muscle contracts

it causes the lower arm to .... and

.... the relaxed biceps muscle.

b Why do muscles work in antagonistic pairs?

shoulder blade

biceps muscle

triceps muscle

7 The diagram shows two sets of arm movements that can be made at the shoulder.

a Work with a partner to identify the antagonistic muscles that cause each set of movements. Try to identify which bones each muscle is attached to.

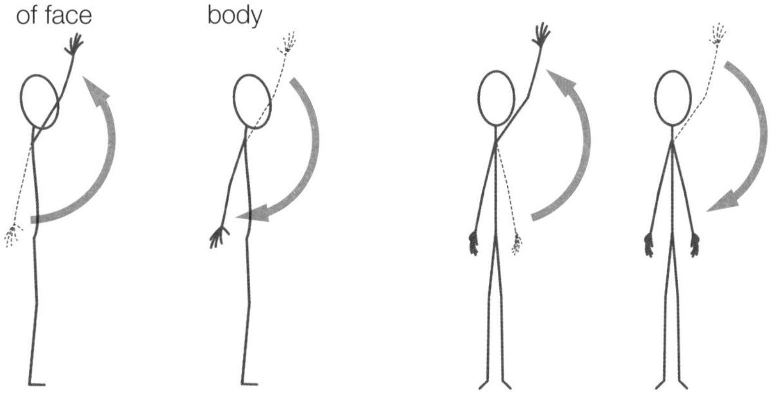

arm in front of face

arm behind body

arm up

arm down

side view

front view

i Muscle moving arm up in front is

attached to ....

and ....

ii Muscle moving arm down behind is

attached to ....

and ....

iii Muscle moving arm up to the side is attached to .... and ....

iv Muscle moving arm down by the side is attached to .... and ....

b Describe one other movement that the arm can make at the shoulder.

1 List as many features of bones as you can.

2 Describe one feature of a real leg that cannot be copied by an artificial leg. Give a reason for your answer.

SB

3 A patient has had their left leg removed just above the knee. In a group, design and build a model prosthesis.

a Evaluate your model, using the table.

Criteria	How easy is it on a scale of 0–4? (0 = not possible, 4 = very easy)
able to stand still	
comfortable when standing still	
feel steady when standing still	
able to walk slowly	
comfortable when walking slowly	
feel steady when walking slowly	

b Use evidence from your table to answer the questions.

i Which feature of the prosthesis was the best? Give a reason for your answer.

ii Which feature of the prosthesis was the least effective? Give a reason for your answer.

iii How could you change the least effective feature to make it more useful?

1a Write M in a box beside a medicine, or R beside a recreational drug.

☐ paracetamol   ☐ cocaine   ☐ salbutamol (in asthma inhalers)

☐ heroin   ☐ ibuprofen   ☐ caffeine (e.g. in coffee)

b Give a reason why all the substances in part **a** are called drugs.

2a What is the useful effect of paracetamol?

b What is its side-effect?

3 Some medicines have depressant effects.

a Describe the effect of a depressant on the nervous system.

b Explain why people taking medicines that have depressant effects may not be allowed to drive.

c Name *one* recreational drug that is a depressant.

4 Explain why some people feel more awake after drinking coffee.

7Ce DRUGS AND SPORT

1 Athletes train to make themselves more fit.

a Describe *one* effect of training on the muscles of the heart.

b Explain why this change in the heart muscles can improve an athlete's performance.

c When running, an athlete breathes more quickly and takes larger breaths than at rest. Give a reason for this.

2 The body makes EPO to increase red blood cell production.

a Where are red blood cells made in the body?

b State the function of red blood cells.

c Describe *one* adaptation of red blood cells for carrying out their function.

d Explain why using EPO would give an athlete an advantage in a competition.

3 Some people ask if athletes should be allowed to use drugs in sport.

a Is this question scientific, non-scientific and/or ethical?

b Give a reason for your answer to part **a**.

4 Explain why stimulant drugs are banned in sports.

1a Olinguitos and humans are mammals. Use your knowledge of human reproduction to predict how an embryo is formed in an olinguito fallopian tube. Include these words in your prediction: fertilisation, gamete, zygote.

b Compare your prediction with a partner to see if you can improve what you have written. If you can, write an improved answer on the lines below.

2 Apart from food, suggest something else that animals need to get from the places in which they live.

3 Olinguito is the name given to organisms of one species.

a Suggest one feature that all olinguitos share.

b Suggest one feature that may vary between different olinguitos.

4a Yanomami people hunt deer for food. The deer eat forest plants. Draw a food chain to show this.

b Suggest what might happen to the Yanomami people if the forest is cut down. Give a reason for your answer.

1 The diagrams show the skulls of a gorilla and a chimpanzee.

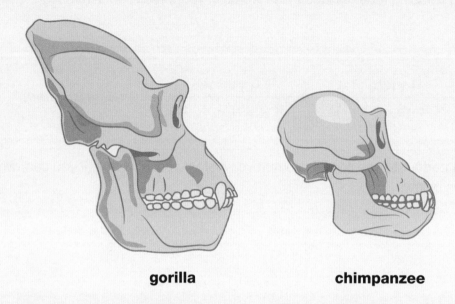

gorilla   chimpanzee

a Describe *one* similarity between the skulls of the two species.

....

b Describe *one* interspecific variation between the skulls.

....

c Suggest *one* feature that would show intraspecific variation in gorilla skulls.

....

d State why gorillas and chimpanzees are separate species.

....

2 Write a number in each box to show how confident you are about the meanings of the following terms.
(0 = do not understand, 4 = very confident)

☐ continuous variation   ☐ discontinuous variation

SB

3 Tick (✓) the correct box for each feature to show if it has continuous or discontinuous variation.

Feature	Continuous	Discontinuous
length of hair	☐	☐
having a scar	☐	☐
height	☐	☐
shoe size	☐	☐
foot length	☐	☐

1 Class A planted broad bean seeds. After one week, they measured the height of each broad bean plant. The results were grouped as shown in this table.

Height (cm)	6.0–7.9	8.0–9.9	10.0–11.9	12.0–13.9	14.0–15.9	16.0–17.9
Number of plants	1	2	6	8	5	1

a Does height show continuous or discontinuous variation? ....

b Give a reason why the data should be displayed in a frequency diagram.

c When plotting these data, should there be spaces between the bar for each height group? Explain your answer.

d State the independent variable in this investigation. ....

e Do the data in the table show a normal distribution? Give a reason for your answer.

2 Students recorded the eye colour of everyone in their class in this table.

Eye colour	brown	grey/blue	green
Number of students	18	11	4

a Does eye colour show continuous or discontinuous variation? ....

b Describe how the data in the eye colour table should be displayed, giving a reason for your answer.

3 The students then measured height and foot length of boys in the class. Their data are shown in this table.

Height (cm)	Foot length (cm)	Height (cm)	Foot length (cm)	Height (cm)	Foot length (cm)
163	23	175	27	181	28
168	27	173	25	168	26
182	27	167	24	176	26
183	28	175	23	175	26

a Plot the results as a scatter graph on the grid below. Show height on the vertical (*y*) axis starting at 160 cm. Show foot length on the horizontal (*x*) axis starting at 20 cm. Label the axes clearly and give the scatter graph a title.

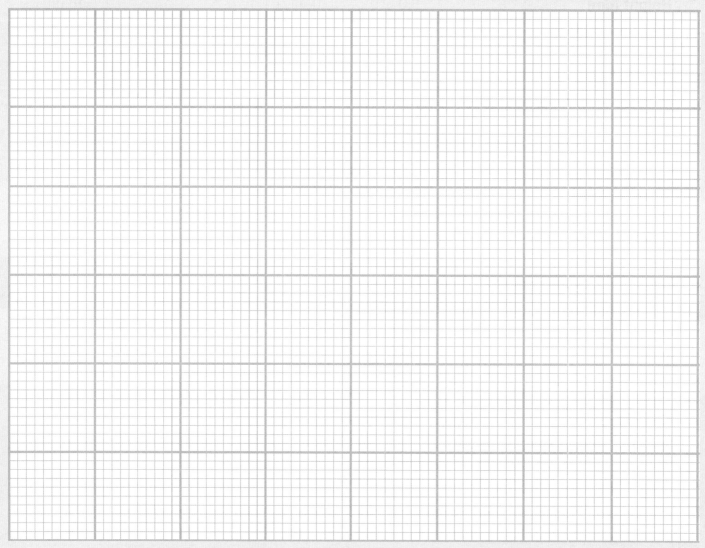

b Draw a line of best fit, and state what it shows.

c Compare your graph with a partner to look for any differences and discuss the difficulties of drawing scatter graphs.

d Write down *two* mistakes that are easy to make when drawing these graphs.

7Db ADAPTATIONS

1a Circle any of the following that are physical environmental (abiotic) factors.

ant	bird	frog	light	temperature	tree	fungus	wind

b Work with a partner to list as many other abiotic factors as you can think of.

2 Draw *one* line from each scientific term to its definition.

Scientific term

adaptation

community

ecosystem

habitat

Definition

the place where an organism lives

all the organisms and abiotic factors in an area

feature that helps an organism survive

all the plants and animals in an area

3 Why do cacti have spines instead of leaves?

4 The diagram shows a water lily.

a Name the habitat of a water lily.

b Explain how one adaptation of this water lily helps it to survive in its habitat.

5 Explain why organisms inherit characteristics from both parents.

1 Bilal found that the cress seedlings he grew in a cupboard were yellow.

a Identify the environmental variation in the seedlings. Give a reason for your answer.

....

b Name the abiotic factor causing the variation. ....

2 Olinguitos are nocturnal animals. What change causes olinguitos to become active?

....

3 Work with a partner to answer the questions from the graph.

a Describe how length of daylight changes in Sodankylä over a year.

How daylength changes by month in Sodankylä (a town in Finland near the Arctic Circle)

b Suggest an adaptation you might see in plants near Sodankylä. Explain how the adaptation helps the plants to survive.

....

....

c Suggest an adaptation you might see in animals near Sodankylä. Explain how the adaptation helps the animals to survive.

....

....

1 The diagram shows a food web in a pond.

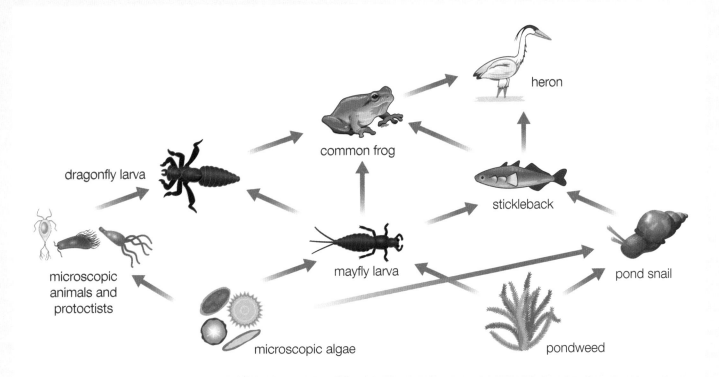

dragonfly larva

common frog

heron

stickleback

microscopic animals and protoctists

mayfly larva

pond snail

microscopic algae

pondweed

a Write down the longest food chain starting at pondweed.

....

b Draw *one* line from each organism to its position in the food web.

Organism

heron

pondweed

mayfly larva

stickleback

Position in food web

producer

prey of frog

carnivore that eats snails

apex predator

c Name *one* species that will be in interspecific competition with sticklebacks for food.

....

2 The olinguito eats fruit and insects.

Tick (✓) *one* box that describes the olinguito.

☐ **A** herbivore

☐ **B** carnivore

☐ **C** insectivore

☐ **D** omnivore

3 Look again at the food web diagram in question **1** on the previous page.

a Choose words from the box to complete the sentences about changes in the food web.
(*Hint:* Not all words are used.)

decrease	increase	intraspecific	interspecific

Two herons feed at the pond. They show _____ competition

for food. The herons eat all the frogs and fish. This could cause the number of pond snails to

_____. The change in number of pond snails could then cause the amount

of pondweed to _____.

b If there are no frogs and fish left, suggest what will happen to the two herons at the pond.

_____

4 The graph shows how snowshoe hare and lynx populations changed over time.

a State what is meant by a population.

_____

_____

b Complete the labelling of the graph on the lines below.

More hares ... means there is more

_____ for

the lynxes. So the lynx population

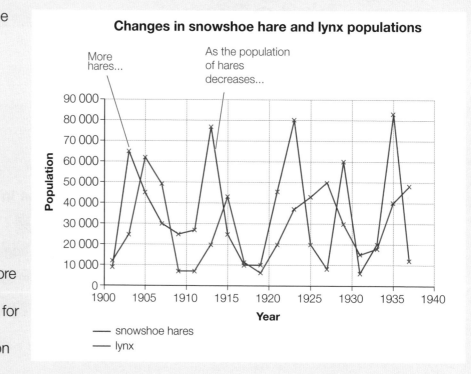

Changes in snowshoe hare and lynx populations

More hares...

As the population of hares decreases...

(y-axis: Population — 0, 10 000, 20 000, 30 000, 40 000, 50 000, 60 000, 70 000, 80 000, 90 000)

(x-axis: Year — 1900, 1905, 1910, 1915, 1920, 1925, 1930, 1935, 1940)

— snowshoe hares
— lynx

_____. As the population of hares decreases ... the population of lynx

_____ because _____

c Suggest *one* reason why the hare population might increase.

_____

_____

1 Complete the boxes to list knowledge you could use to plan a 'green' 18-storey apartment block in a city in your country.

plants living near the city	animals living near the city
resources needed by plants and animals	**climate in the city** temperature: max. min. rainfall daylength

b Draw a circle round the most useful knowledge in the table for greening the apartment block.

2 Draw a design for the tower block in the space below. Label each of your 'green' suggestions.

1a Look at this food chain: lettuce → caterpillar → sparrow → sparrowhawk

Draw *one* line from each organism to its trophic level in the food chain.

Organism	Trophic level
lettuce	secondary consumer
caterpillar	top consumer
sparrow	primary consumer
sparrowhawk	producer

2 The energy stored in a caterpillar passes to the sparrow that eats it. Which part of this energy can be passed on to the sparrowhawk that eats the sparrow? Tick (✓) *one* box.

☐ **A** energy stored in undigested food that passes out of the sparrow
☐ **B** energy released by respiration to keep the sparrow warm
☐ **C** energy stored in substances in the sparrow's tissues
☐ **D** energy released by respiration to allow the sparrow to move

3 DDT is a persistent pesticide, which kills insects.

a Give a reason why a farmer might want to use DDT. ....

....

b Give the reason why earthworms underground come into contact with DDT. Explain why?

....

....

c Blackbirds eat earthworms, and peregrine falcons eat blackbirds. DDT causes thinning of bird egg shells. Explain why the peregrine falcon population decreased in the 1970s but the blackbird population did not. You can use the space at the bottom of the page for a diagram, if you wish.

....

....

....

4 In a garden food chain, 1 fox eats 5 rabbits. The rabbits eat 20 lettuces.
You will use this information to draw a pyramid of numbers on the grid below.

a First, decide a suitable scale to fit the 20 producers across the page. Divide a useful width of the grid by 20. You will use this scale for all the bars.

scale: 1 cm across the grid = _____ individuals

b Draw the lettuces bar at the bottom of the grid, making sure it is the correct width for your scale. All your bars should be the same height. Label the lettuces bar and mark the middle at the top of the bar.

c Use your scale to calculate the width of the rabbit bar. Add this, making sure it is centred on top of the lettuce bar. Label the bar.

d Use the same method to draw and label the fox bar on top of the rabbit bar.

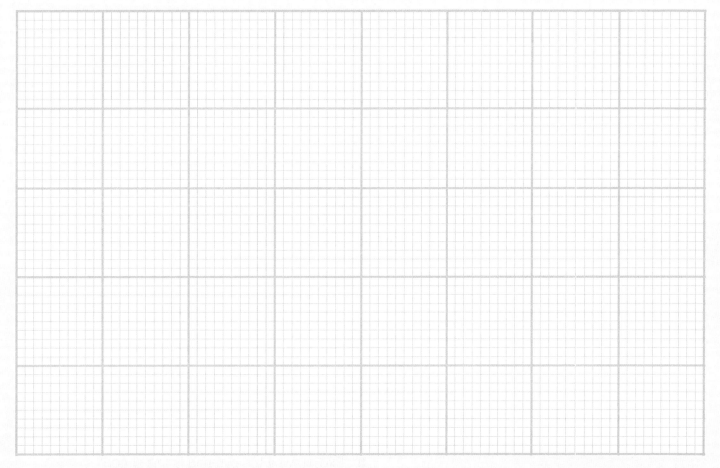

e Compare your pyramid with that of a partner. Mark any corrections needed to make your pyramid better.

5 Fleas are insect parasites of rabbits. Explain why this pyramid of numbers is not shaped like a pyramid.

| fleas |
| rabbit |
| lettuce plants |

1 Give *one* example of each of the following.

ai a herbivore _____ **ii** a carnivore _____

b a predator and its prey _____

ci biotic factor _____ **ii** abiotic factor _____

2 Check your answers to question **1** with a partner and discuss any differences. If you agree a better answer, add it in a different colour.

SB

3 Is having measles an example of continuous or discontinuous variation? Explain your reasoning.

_____

_____

4 In cold regions, many mammals hibernate (sleep) through winter. Describe two advantages of hibernation.

i _____

ii _____

5 Complete the text with words from the box.

population	community	habitat	ecosystem	species

Organisms that share many similar features are grouped as a _____.

The place where the organisms live is called their _____. All the individuals

of a species living in an area form a _____. All the different species living in

an area form a _____. All the organisms and the environmental factors that

affect them in an area is the _____.

6a Herons eat bristlenose fish, and bristlenose fish eat microscopic algae. Label this pyramid of numbers for this food chain.

b Explain why the pyramid is this shape.

_____

_____

1a Write S for solid, L for liquid or G for gas in the box beside each substance.

☐ carbon dioxide   ☐ cooking oil   ☐ gravel   ☐ oxygen

☐ plastic   ☐ sand   ☐ water

b Describe how you can tell the difference between solids, liquids and gases.

_____

_____

2a Check your answers to question **1a** with a partner. Mark any corrections in a different colour.

b Discuss with your partner how to improve your answer to question **1b**. Write your improved answer below.

_____

_____

_____

3 Sea water is a solution of water and dissolved substances, such as salt.

a Explain what *solution* means.

_____

_____

b Tick (✓) *one* box to show how you would separate the dissolved substances from the sea water.
☐ **A** filtering
☐ **B** evaporating
☐ **C** sieving
☐ **D** diluting

c Give a reason for your answer to part **b**.

_____

4 Can gases dissolve? Explain how you can tell.

_____

_____

SB 1 Explain why filtering could help analyse where a soil sample comes from.

SB 2 The table shows the steps in a method for filtering a sand and water mixture.

Method	Corrections to method
A Fold a circular filter paper in half.	
B Fold the filter paper in half again to form a triangle shape.	
C Open out one layer of the paper to form a cone.	
D Place the filter paper cone into a filter funnel.	
E Stir the sand mixture with water so that all the sand is suspended.	
F Place the filter funnel into the neck of a conical flask.	
G Pour the sand and water into the filter paper.	

As you carry out the method, check that each step is written as clearly as it can be.

a Write any corrections to make a step clearer in the right column.

b Use arrows to indicate any steps that should be moved into another order.

c In the space below, draw any diagrams that would make something clearer.

1 Draw *one* line from each scientific term to its definition.

Scientific term	Definition
suspension	two or more substances jumbled up together
colloid	a liquid containing dissolved substances
mixture	a liquid containing small insoluble pieces that sink slowly
solution	a liquid containing small insoluble pieces that do not sink

2 Why is waste water (e.g. in drains) an example of a mixture?

_____

_____

3a Tick (✓) *one* box for each substance to show what type of mixture it is.

Substance	Solution	Colloid	Suspension
milk	☐	☐	☐
sea water	☐	☐	☐
Styrofoam™	☐	☐	☐
fizzy drink	☐	☐	☐
paint	☐	☐	☐
fog	☐	☐	☐

b Write down one other example of each type of mixture.

solution _____

colloid _____

suspension _____

4 How confident are you in your answers to question **3**?
Complete the face to show your confidence – the bigger the smile, the more confident you are.

5 Which type of mixture is transparent? Tick (✓) one box.

☐ **A** colloid
☐ **B** solution
☐ **C** suspension
☐ **D** none of the above (they are all opaque)

6a Complete the labels on the diagram using scientific terms where you can.

b Ask a partner to say how many of your labels they think could be improved. Make any improvements in a different colour. Then, in a group, discuss and finalise your labels in another different colour.

7 In water treatment to produce drinking water, waste water is first filtered then settled. Cross out the wrong word to show if these statement about the liquid taken from settlement ponds are true or false.

a Water from the settlement ponds is pure. **true / false**

b Water from the settlement ponds contains dissolved substances. **true / false**

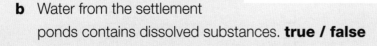

8 Draw a flow chart below to summarise the stages of water treatment. For each stage, name the process used to clean the water.

1 Choose words from the box to complete the sentences.

insoluble	soluble	solute	solution	solvent

Nail polish does not dissolve in water, so we say it is .... in water.

Propanone is used in nail polish remover, and nail polish is .... in

propanone.

When propanone dissolves nail polish, the propanone is the .... of the

solution that is formed, and the nail polish is the ....

2a 20 g of sugar is stirred into 150 g of tea. What is the mass of the solution formed?

....

b Explain your answer to part **a**.

....

....

3 State what is meant by the concentration of a solution.

....

....

....

4 The solubility of blue copper sulfate is 32 g per 100 g of water at 20 °C.

a State the largest mass of copper sulfate that would dissolve in 500 g of water at 20 °C.

....

b Explain your answer to part **a**.

....

....

c Explain what you could do to 100 g water so that it dissolved more than 32 g of copper sulfate.

....

....

....

1 Draw and colour the flame of a Bunsen burner for each air hole position.

air hole
closed

air hole
half open

air hole
fully open

2 Tick (✓) *one* box in each row to show which type of Bunsen flame is described.

Description	Roaring blue	Medium blue	Yellow
safety flame	☐	☐	☐
for heating tubes of liquid	☐	☐	☐
hottest above pale blue cone	☐	☐	☐
leaves sooty layer on surfaces	☐	☐	☐

SB

3 Explain why the air hole of a Bunsen burner should be closed before the gas is lit.

4 State a hazard for each of the following when working with a Bunsen burner.

a recently used Bunsen burner

b combustible materials, such as hair

c split gas hose

5 Explain why a Bunsen burner is useful for evaporating a solution to dryness.

6 Describe a safe way to light a Bunsen burner.

7 Work with a partner to complete these safety instructions for heating copper sulfate solution to dryness.

a Place the Bunsen burner on a .... before lighting it.

b Only use a .... flame to heat the solution.

c When not using the Bunsen burner, ...

d Always wear .... while heating.

e Fill the evaporating basin only .... with solution before heating.

f Hold or move hot apparatus using ....

g When most of the water has evaporated, ...

8 Compare your answers to question **7** with other students. Mark any corrections to your answers in a different colour.

9 Give two reasons why a medium blue flame is used for heating to dryness.

i ....

ii ....

1 Choose the correct words from the box to complete the text.

| concentrated | dilute | gas | liquid | solid | solute | solvent |

Evaporation of a solution happens when the _____ changes from

a _____ to a _____, and escapes into

the air. This leaves the _____ behind in a solution that gets more

_____. When evaporation is complete, _____ crystals

of the solute are left in the dish.

SB

2 Would the rate of evaporation of water be greater in a cold cave or in a warm salt pond? Explain your answer.

_____

_____

3a The boiling point of ethanol is 78 °C. State what this means.

_____

b Some water was heated to boiling. The temperature at boiling was 100.5 °C. What can be said about the water? Give a reason for your answer.

_____

_____

SB

4 Explain how a mixture of 50% ethanol and 50% water changes when heated to 80 °C.

_____

_____

5a Describe how you could produce table salt from rock salt.

_____

_____

_____

b Discuss your answer with a partner, then mark any improvements in a different colour.

1 Which of these separations could be done by chromatography? Tick (✓) *one* box.
   ☐ **A** sand separated from a sand/gravel mixture
   ☐ **B** all the solids separated from a mixture of solids and a liquid
   ☐ **C** individual solutes separated from a solvent
   ☐ **D** all the solvents together separated from a solute

2 Look at the diagram. Describe how this experiment was set up.

chromatography
paper

beaker

pencil line

solvent

black   brown   red   green   blue   orange

....

....

....

....

....

....

....

3 The diagram shows the results of chromatography using food dyes.

a Which colour was carried the fastest? ....

b Write down *one* other conclusion from the results.

....

....

....

....

blue   red   yellow   green

c As a group, discuss your conclusions.
   Write down another correct conclusion from your discussions.

....

....

....

1 Use words from the box to complete the text.

condensation	desalination	distillation	evaporation

The process of removing dissolved solutes from sea water to make it suitable for drinking is

called _____ . One way of doing this is to heat the water. This causes

_____ of the water to form steam. The steam is then cooled, causing

_____ of the water to form a liquid again. This method is known as

_____ .

SB

2 Why do many parts of the world need sources of water different from the ones used in the United Kingdom?

SB

3 One of the products of distilling sea water is drinking water. Suggest another product from this process. Explain your answer.

4 The diagram shows a simple set-up for distilling sea water.

a One hazard with this apparatus is suck-back. Describe suck-back and suggest how it can be avoided.

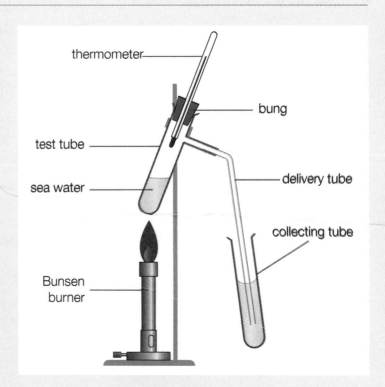

b Describe how risk from one other hazard with this apparatus can be reduced.

5 The diagram shows another set-up for simple distillation in the lab.

a Name the part labelled A in the diagram.

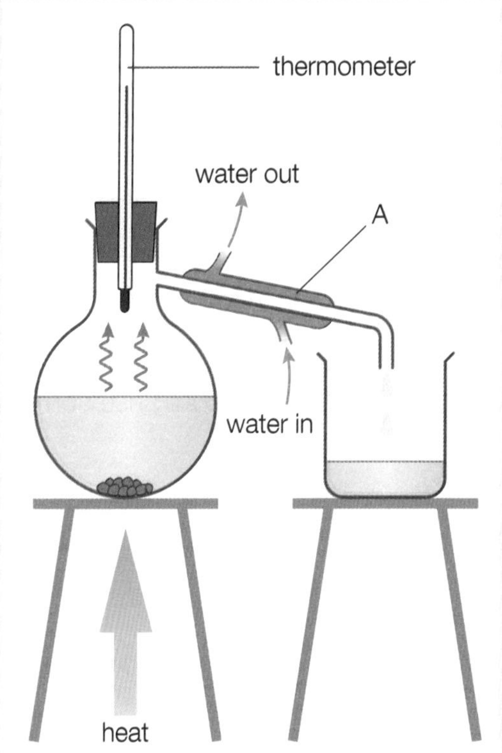

....

thermometer

water out

A

water in

heat

b Explain the effect of using this set-up for distillation compared with the apparatus shown in question **4**.

....

....

....

....

c Suggest how you could test whether the liquid collected is pure.

....

....

6 Explain why a solar-powered water still might be useful:

a on a ship that has broken down at sea

....

....

b in a country where the drinking water contains bacteria that cause diseases.

....

....

1 Draw *one* line from each method to what it separates.

Method		Separates
filtering		separates out a mixture of solutes (from a solution)
evaporation		separates the solvent from a solution
chromatography		separates solids from a liquid
distillation		separates all the solutes from a solution

2 An earthquake damages the drinking water supply in an area. The only source of water is a dirty pond.

a Describe how you could use some thin fabric to remove the mud from the water.

....

b The diagram shows an emergency solar still.

Explain how the still could produce safe drinking water from the pond water.

transparent cover

pond water

drinking water

....

....

....

....

....

c Suggest why it might be a good idea to boil the water produced from the still before cooling and drinking it.

....

d State the apparatus you would use to test if the water was pure, and describe how you would use it.

....

....

....

7Fa CHEMISTRY IN THE HOME

1 Identify which of these two children is more likely to be harmed. Explain your reasoning.

2 Name three uses of chemical substances in the home.

i

ii

iii

B 3 State two ways in which young children might have an accident with bleach.

i

ii

B 4 Suggest two ways to reduce the risk of young children being hurt by bleach.

i

ii

5 Complete these sentences, if you can.

a Acidic foods taste _____ .

b Very acidic foods are _____ for your teeth.

c Some alkalis are hazardous because they are _____ .

d We show how acidic or alkaline something is using _____ .

7Fa HAZARDS

SB

1 Write down one acid used in the laboratory and one acid found in the home.

Acid used in the laboratory ....

Acid found in the home ....

2 Describe what is meant by a hazardous substance.

....

....

3 Look at this list of acids.

A concentrated sulfuric acid	**B** dilute citric acid	**C** dilute hydrochloric acid

a Write down the letter of the acid which is safe to drink. ....

b Describe what this acid would taste like. ....

....

4 Draw *one* line from each substance to show where it is usually found.

Substance   **Where it is found**

ethanoic acid (acetic)   in household cleaners

dilute sodium hydroxide

dilute nitric acid

ammonia   in foods

citric acid

dilute sulfuric acid

caustic soda (sodium hydroxide)   in laboratories

dilute hydrochloric acid

SB

5 Which international hazard symbols will be displayed on the following household chemicals? Choose letters from the box.

A dangerous to the environment	**B** toxic	**C** corrosive
D explosive	**E** flammable	**F** caution

a turpentine – damages pond life, causes headaches and sickness, can catch fire if heated

....

b soap powder – causes irritation to the skin ....

1 Circle three hazards in the picture above. For each one suggest a way of reducing the risk of harm.

i ....

....

ii ....

....

iii ....

....

2 Look at the method below and answer the questions.

A| Measure 10 cm³ of dilute hydrochloric acid into a test tube.

B| Use a dropper to add 10 drops of beetroot juice to the acid.

C| Record any change in colour of the beetroot juice.

D| Tidy away your apparatus.

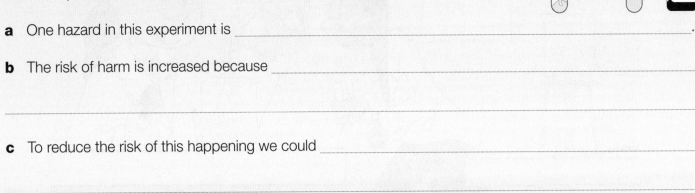

Now complete these sentences:

a One hazard in this experiment is _____ .

b The risk of harm is increased because _____

_____

c To reduce the risk of this happening we could _____

_____

3 The table shows a 'confidence grid'. Tick ✓ *one* box for each statement in the table.

Statement	Definitely correct	Might be correct	Might be wrong	Definitely wrong
a Used to show that a substance is corrosive				
b Used to show that a substance is dangerous to the environment				
c Used to show that a substance is flammable				
d Used to show that a substance is a health hazard				
e Used to show that a substance is toxic				

4 Where you think that the statements in question **3** are wrong, suggest what the symbol actually means.

_____

_____

1 Draw *one* line from each substance to the term that best describes it.

Substance   **Description**

pure water

                                            acid

hydrochloric acid

                                            alkali

sugar solution

                                            neutral

oven cleaner

2 Complete this table:

Solution	Colour of litmus		Colour of red cabbage indicator	Acid, alkali or neutral?
	Red litmus	**Blue litmus**		
lemon juice	red	red	red	
toothpaste			purple	
pure water	red	blue	pink	
vinegar				acid
soap solution	blue	blue		

3 These steps for making an indicator have been written in the wrong order. Write the correct order in the space provided:

Correct order:

A| Crush the mixture

B| Add red cabbage leaves

C| Mix water and ethanol

D| Stir

E| Collect the liquid indicator

F| Filter the mixture

4 A few drops of litmus solution are added to some toothpaste. The litmus turns blue. What does this tell you about the toothpaste?

5 An indicator called methyl orange turns red in acids and yellow in alkalis. Another indicator called phenolphthalein (pronounced *feen-ol-**fthay**-leen*) turns colourless in acids but pink in alkalis.

SB

a What colour would methyl orange turn with oven cleaner?

....

b What colour would phenolphthalein turn with oven cleaner?

....

6 Complete the table below by choosing substances that would give all the results in each row of the table.

Substance	Colour of red litmus	Colour of blue litmus	Colour of methyl orange	Colour of universal indicator
	red	blue	orange	green
	red	red	red	red
	blue	blue	yellow	purple
	red	red	red	orange
	blue	blue	yellow	dark green

7 Find out about another indicator and describe how it changes with acids and alkalis.

....

....

....

1 State where these acids and alkalis are likely to be found. Choose your answer from *laboratory, food* or *household cleaners*.

a dilute sulfuric acid ....

b caustic soda (sodium hydroxide) ....

c dilute sodium hydroxide ....

d citric acid ....

e ammonia ....

f dilute hydrochloric acid ....

g ethanoic acid (acetic acid) ....

h dilute nitric acid ....

2 Complete this table:

Name of chemical	Colour of universal indicator	Acidic, alkaline or neutral	pH number
	red	very acidic	1
water		neutral	
sodium hydroxide solution			14
carbon dioxide solution		not very acidic	

3 Tick (✓) the sentence below that *best* explains what pH means.
☐ **A** pH is a way of measuring how acidic or alkaline a liquid is.
☐ **B** pH tells you whether or not a liquid is an acid.
☐ **C** pH tells you whether or not a liquid is an alkali.
☐ **D** pH is used to show if a liquid is dangerous or not.

4 Draw *one* line to link each substance to its pH.

Substance	pH
toothpaste	1
sulfuric acid	5
oven cleaner	7
rainwater	9
salt solution	13

5 Describe two ways of measuring the pH of a solution.

i ....

ii ....

6 Write down as much detail as you can about what the pH of a liquid tells us about how hazardous that liquid is likely to be.

....

....

....

7 Describe and explain one way in which measuring pH can help us to protect the environment.

....

....

....

....

8 Look at your answers to question **5** on page 63. If you can, write better answers below.

....

....

....

1 Tick (✓) the statement that *best* describes what neutralisation is.

☐ **A** an acid cancelling out an alkali

☐ **B** an alkali cancelling out an acid

☐ **C** the reaction between an acid and a base to form a salt and water only

☐ **D** a mixture of an acid and an alkali becoming more neutral

2 A student adds sodium hydroxide to hydrochloric acid, and evaporates the solution.

a Give the chemical name of the solid left behind. _____

b The student wants to put this solid on some food. Suggest *one* reason why this is not a good idea.

_____

_____

c Suggest how the student could check that the solution is neutral without adding anything to the solution.

_____

_____

_____

3 Complete these word equations.

a lithium hydroxide + hydrochloric acid → _____ + _____

b _____ + sulfuric acid → sodium sulfate + _____

c sodium hydroxide + hydrochloric acid → _____ + _____

d lithium hydroxide + sulfuric acid → _____ + _____

4a Write the word equation for the reaction between citric acid and sodium hydroxide. The salt is a citrate.

b Label each substance in your equation using *two* words from the box.

| alkaline | acidic | neutral | product | reactant |

7Fd THE CHEMICAL INDUSTRY (STEM)

SB **1** Name *four* products of the chemical industry.

2 Two factories produce the same bleach. Some of their quality control analysis is shown below.

Time of sample	Factory A	Factory B
	pH of product X	pH of product X
02:00	12.5	12.8
04:00	12.6	12.4
06:00	12.5	12.5
08:00	12.5	12.5
10:00	12.6	12.6
12:00	12.6	12.4
14:00	12.5	12.6
16:00	12.5	12.5
18:00	12.5	12.7
20:00	12.6	12.4
22:00	12.5	12.8
24:00	12.5	12.8

a Describe how you would use universal indicator to measure the pH of a sample of bleach in the laboratory.

b Give *one* reason why a factory would use a pH meter instead.

c Imagine you are the quality control technician in charge of both factories. Explain which factory's production line you would shut.

7Fe NEUTRALISATION IN DAILY LIFE

1 Complete this word equation, which shows how magnesium hydroxide (an antacid) neutralises stomach acid:

magnesium hydroxide + ... acid → .... + water

2 Explain why a coal power station sprays waste gases with calcium hydroxide. To answer this, tick (✓) *one* box for each of parts **a** and **b** below.

a They do this:
- ☐ **A** to cool the gases.
- ☐ **B** to stop the gases leaving the power station.
- ☐ **C** to make table salt.
- ☐ **D** to reduce pollution.

b This is because calcium hydroxide:
- ☐ **A** is a base, which neutralises acidic waste gases.
- ☐ **B** is an acid, which neutralises alkaline waste gases.
- ☐ **C** is a base that reacts with acids to form sodium chloride.
- ☐ **D** is a very cold substance, mined in the Arctic.

3 Write a word equation for the reaction between calcium hydroxide and the acid gas released by power stations.

.... + ... → .... + ...

4 Which *two* of these substances react to make potassium sulfate?

hydrochloric acid, sulfuric acid, nitric acid, calcium hydroxide, sodium hydroxide, potassium hydroxide.

....

5 Indigestion tablets reduce acidity in the stomach. Write down the steps for an experiment to find out which indigestion tablets work best.

....

....

....

....

7Fe DANGER AT HOME

1a Complete this general word equation.

acid + alkali → _____ + _____

b This type of reaction is called a _____ reaction.

2 Complete these word equations:

a hydrochloric acid + sodium hydroxide → _____ + _____

b sulfuric acid + potassium hydroxide → _____ + _____

c nitric acid + sodium hydroxide → _____ + _____

d hydrochloric acid + calcium hydroxide → _____ + _____

SB

3 Two of the chemicals a student mixed, before they got hot, were sodium hydroxide (drain cleaner) and sulfuric acid (rust remover).

a What was the sign that a chemical reaction had taken place?

_____

b What do you call the type of reaction that occurs between these two substances?

_____

c Write a word equation for the reaction that occurs.

_____

4 A student tested some substances and recorded their results in the table below. Tick (✓) *one* column to indicate the type of each substance.

Name of substance	Does it dissolve in water?	Does it react with acid?	Type of substance		
			Insoluble base	**Alkali**	**Neither**
A	Yes	Yes			
B	Yes	No			
C	No	No			
D	No	Yes			
E	Yes	No			

7Ga SORTING RUBBISH

1 Give two reasons why we need to recycle more of our waste.

i ....

....

ii ....

2 What are the three states of matter?

....

3a Name the state of matter that waste plastic is in.

....

b Which other waste materials are in this state of matter? Tick (✓) the boxes that apply.
- ☐ carbon dioxide
- ☐ paper
- ☐ vegetable oil
- ☐ paint
- ☐ aluminium
- ☐ glass

4a Work in a small group to discuss the differences between solids and liquids. Describe two differences between solids and liquids. Write your answer in the first box. Ignore the second box for now.

Ideas from my group:

....

....

....

What we now think:

....

....

....

b Describe a similarity between solids and liquids.

7Ga SOLIDS, LIQUIDS AND GASES

1 Look at the three syringes containing a solid, a liquid and a gas.

a Which syringe behaves differently from the other two? ....

b Explain how and why it behaves differently.

....

....

....

sand   water   air

2 Tick (✓) the boxes to show which states of matter have which properties.

State of matter	Properties			
	Keeps its shape	Keeps its volume	Able to be compressed	Able to flow
solid				
liquid				
gas				

3 A gas has a density of 0.002 g/cm³.

a State the mass of the gas in a volume of 1 cm³. Mass = ... g.

b Calculate the mass of 30 cm³ of this gas. ....

Mass = ... g.

c 30 cm³ of the gas is compressed and now has a density of 0.009 g/cm³. State the mass of the gas.

Mass = ... g.

4a Burning fossil fuels produce acidic gases. Some of these gases have been dissolved in water.
Tick *one* (✓) box to select which pH that the solution is likely to be.

☐ **A** pH 1   ☐ **B** pH 7   ☐ **C** pH 7.5   ☐ **D** pH 13

b Identify the chemical test that you would use to find the pH of the solution.

1 Making a hypothesis is an important part of scientific method.

a What is a hypothesis?

b Tick (✓) the statement that is a possible hypothesis.
- ☐ **A** Salty water takes longer to boil than tap water.
- ☐ **B** If I add more salt to water, then the boiling point will decrease.
- ☐ **C** The boiling point of water depends on the amount of salt in it.
- ☐ **D** Sea water will take longer to boil than salty water.

2 Complete the following sentences, only using the words *hypothesis* and *data*.

After an experiment has been carried out, you consider the

_____ that you have collected. If

the _____ matches the prediction,

this is evidence that the _____ is

correct. We say that the _____

supports the _____. When

_____ from many experiments supports

the _____, it becomes a theory.

3a State two things that make a good theory.

i _____

ii _____

b What is the difference between a hypothesis and a theory?

_____

_____

_____

4 Complete the flow diagram to outline the different stages in scientific method.

Observation and question

→

_____

↓

_____

↓

New hypothesis needed

_____

↓

_____

↓

Data match prediction?

No

Yes

Hypothesis looks correct

B

5 Look at the drawings. They show a room before and after the fire has been lit. There is a balloon in the room. Work in groups to answer the questions below.

a Write an observation about what is happening to the balloon.

b Write a question that you could ask about the balloon.

c Write a hypothesis about what affects the balloon. Use the phrase 'depends on'.

d Design an experiment to test your hypothesis. Outline what you will do.

e If your hypothesis is correct, describe what you expect to observe happening in your experiment. Make a prediction.

7Gb PARTICLES

1 The particle model states that all matter is made up of tiny particles. What else does it state? Tick (✓) *three* correct sentences.

- ☐ **A** All matter is made up of gas.
- ☐ **B** Particles move all the time.
- ☐ **C** Particles can only vibrate in one direction.
- ☐ **D** Forces keep the particles far apart.
- ☐ **E** There are forces of attraction holding the particles together.
- ☐ **F** The forces between particles are always the same strength.
- ☐ **G** Forces vary in strength for different states of matter.

2 Look at the drawings. Label each state of matter.

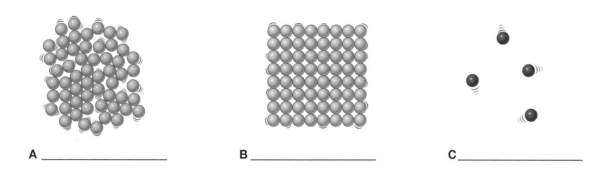

A _____   B _____   C _____

3 Fill in the table below to describe the particles in solids, liquids and gases.

State of matter	Arrangement of particles	Movement of particles	Strength of forces between particles	Example
Solid			strong	
Liquid	fairly close together			
Gas		move in all directions		

SB

4 How does the particle theory explain:

a why gases can be compressed but liquids cannot

....

....

....

b why gases spread out to fill a container

....

....

....

c why sugar disappears when stirred into some water?

....

....

....

5 Look at your answer to Question **4a** on page 75. Discuss in your group what you have learned about particle theory. If you can, write a better answer in the lower box.

6 Explain what you see when a tea bag is dropped into a beaker of cold water and left for two weeks.

To answer this, tick (✓) *one* answer for each of parts **a** and **b** below.

a What happens:
- ☐ **A** The tea bag and the water do not change.
- ☐ **B** The tea bag gets bigger and bigger.
- ☐ **C** A brown colour slowly spreads through the water.
- ☐ **D** The tea bag dissolves and the tea falls out.

b This is because:
- ☐ **A** the forces between tea particles are weak when it is cold.
- ☐ **B** particles only move when it is hot.
- ☐ **C** the brown tea particles are constantly moving.
- ☐ **D** liquids have no fixed shape.

1 Explain the Brownian motion of a soot speck. To answer this, tick (✓) *one* box for each of parts **a** and **b** below.

a Brownian motion is when the speck:
- ☐ **A** vibrates backwards and forwards.
- ☐ **B** moves jerkily in many different directions.
- ☐ **C** moves smoothly in one direction.
- ☐ **D** moves jerkily in one direction.

b It happens because the speck:
- ☐ **A** is hit by air particles moving in random directions.
- ☐ **B** is hit by air particles moving in one direction.
- ☐ **C** is in constant motion, and always vibrating.
- ☐ **D** is hot.

2 Complete the following sentences, using only the words in the box below.

Brownian	data	experiment	particle	theory	prediction	test

Pollen grains in water move by _____ motion. Albert Einstein developed

a hypothesis to explain this. This was based on the _____ theory,

which was not generally accepted by scientists at that time. He used his hypothesis to make

a _____ about how far a pollen grain would be moved by water. An

_____ was then carried out to _____ the hypothesis.

The _____ matched the prediction and provided evidence to support the

particle _____ .

3a 1 nanometre is 0.000 000 001 metres. How many nanometres are in a metre? _____

b Why is it not sensible to measure a football pitch in nanometres?

_____

_____

c In a group, think of *two* things that should be measured in nanometres?

_____

_____

7Gd DIFFUSION

1 Drawing X shows gas particles in a box, which is separated into two sections. A tiny hole is made in the barrier. Complete drawing Y to show the positions of the gas particles after a long period of time.

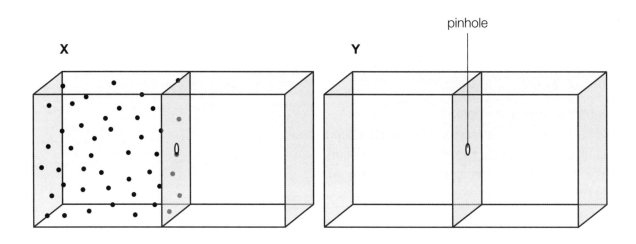

pinhole

X

Y

2 Explain what happens during the diffusion of a gas. To answer this, tick (✓) *one* box for each of parts **a** and **b** below.

a During diffusion:
- ☐ **A** a gas spreads out.
- ☐ **B** a gas moves from one place to another.
- ☐ **C** a gas takes up a smaller volume.
- ☐ **D** a gas increases in density.

b This is because:
- ☐ **A** particles of a gas move in the same direction.
- ☐ **B** particles of a gas move in random directions.
- ☐ **C** particles of a gas stay still.
- ☐ **D** particles of a gas move more slowly.

3 Complete the following sentences, only using the words *particles*, *liquids* and *gases*.

Diffusion is caused by the movement of _____ into spaces between other

_____ . It occurs more slowly in liquids than in gases. This is because the

_____ in _____ are closer together and cannot move

as freely as the _____ in _____ .

4 Think about what happens when you add sugar to a hot drink and do not stir it. Use particle theory to explain why this makes the drink taste sweet.

_____

_____

_____

7Ge AIR PRESSURE

B

1 How can air produce a pressure?

2a Use the particle model to explain why an inflated balloon keeps its shape.

b Give the reason why the density of the gas in the balloon increases when you squeeze it. (Be careful not to pop it though!)

c What will happen to the pressure in the balloon when it is squashed?

d Why might the balloon pop if you squash it too much?

3 The drawing shows a cross section of a balloon and the air molecules inside and outside it. Which statement is correct? Tick (✓) *one* box.
   ☐ **A** The gas pressure inside the balloon is greater than outside it.
   ☐ **B** The balloon is deflating.
   ☐ **C** There is a vacuum inside the balloon.
   ☐ **D** There are more particles hitting the outside of the balloon than the inside.

4a What is a vacuum?

b Describe how a vacuum can cause something to implode (get squashed in on itself)?

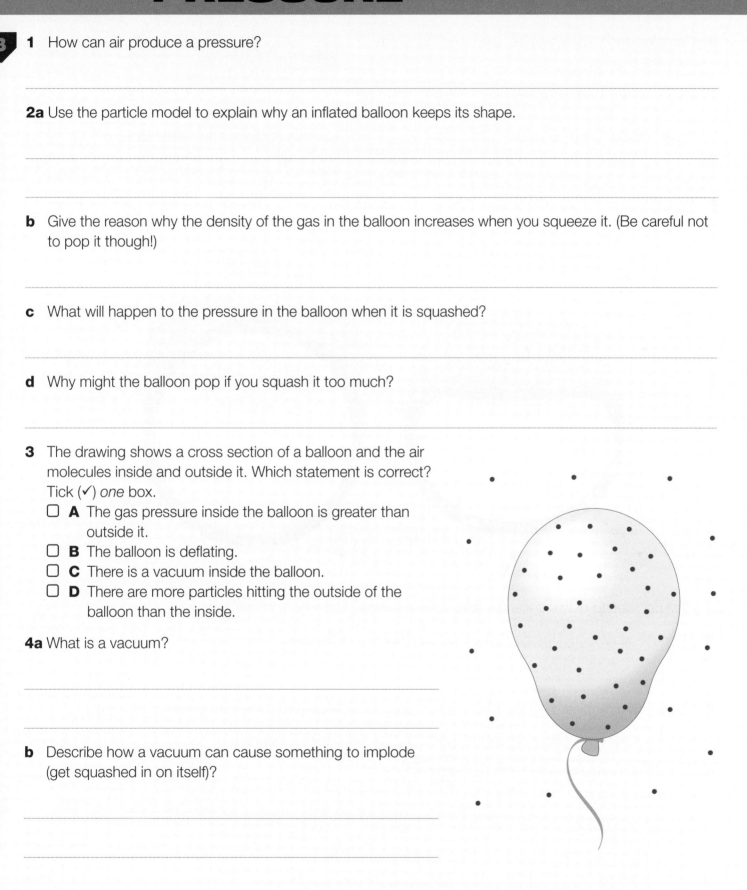

5 Complete the following sentences using the words from the box.

greater	inside	less	outside

When you suck the straw, there is _____ pressure _____

the straw. So, the air pressure _____ the straw acting on the liquid is

_____ than the pressure inside the straw and the liquid is pushed up the straw.

6 Drawings X and Y show two tyres. One is inflated and the other is deflated (flat). Not all particles have been shown.

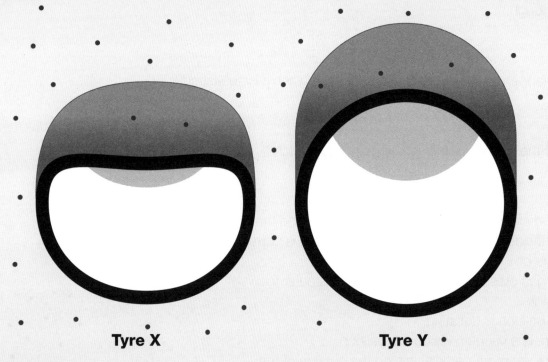

Tyre X　　　　　　　　　　**Tyre Y**

a Add particles to drawing X and a label to explain why the tyre is soft and floppy.

b Describe what would happen if the tyre has a very small puncture.

c Share your completed diagram with others. Discuss whether the labelled diagrams in your group:

- are correct
- show enough information
- are easy to understand.

d Write down *two* ways in which your diagram is good.

e Write down *one* thing that you could improve about your diagram.

1 Add symbols to the maps to represent the weather forecast shown. Include a key.

> It will be a sunny morning in the north, and a cloudy afternoon with heavy rain. The south will have some sunshine and some rain, and a dry, cloudy afternoon. Strong winds will blow from the south all day.

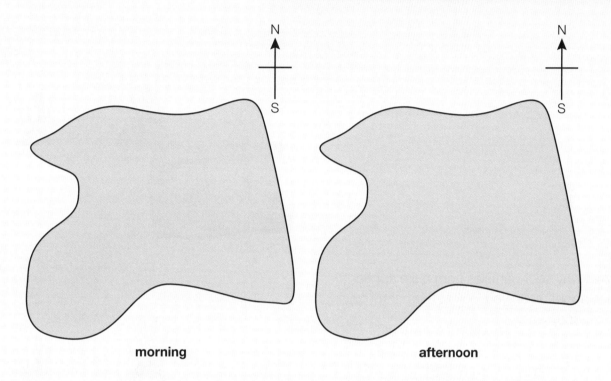

morning   afternoon

2 The table shows the air pressures in two locations, X and Y. For each row of the table, show which way the wind blows (X to Y or Y to X) by drawing an arrow in the central box.

Pressure at X (kPa)	Wind direction	Pressure at Y (kPa)
100		130
125		113
129		122
160		190

3 Meteorologists use symbols to communicate things. Explain how the symbols you have used in question **1** help explain what the wind is like.

....

....

....

1   Describe solids, liquids and gases in terms of the movement of their particles and the forces between the particles.

a   a solid

_____

b   a liquid

_____

_____

c   a gas

_____

_____

X

SB

2   Explain why soot particles from a fire appear to dance about when you look at them through a microscope.

_____

_____

_____

_____

Y

3   Poisonous waste has leaked from a landfill site into a pond. Draw particles in the ponds in diagrams Y and Z to show what will happen to the poison in the pond over time.

4   Tick (✓) the statement that is a hypothesis.

☐ A   There seems to be a lot of methane produced in the landfill site.

☐ B   The amount of methane depends on the amount of rotting waste.

☐ C   If we increase the amount of rotting waste, then more methane is produced.

☐ D   Why is so much methane produced in a landfill site?

Z

1 The diagram shows how water changes from one state to another.

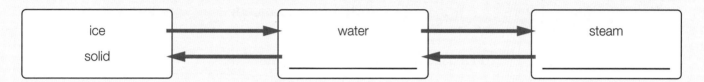

| ice | | water | | steam |
| solid | | | | |

Add the names of the states to the boxes.

Label the arrows to show the physical changes (the changes of state).

2 Sea water is a solution of dissolved substances such as salt. What does the term solution mean?

....

....

3 We can use changes of state to separate materials from mixtures. Which change of state would you use to separate salt from sea water?

....

4 During evaporation, a liquid turns into a gas. Tick (✓) the statements that are true:
- ☐ **A** Liquids *only* evaporate once the boiling point has been reached.
- ☐ **B** During evaporation, particles leave the liquid as a gas.
- ☐ **C** Evaporation gets faster as the liquid gets hotter.
- ☐ **D** Evaporation only occurs when it is warm.
- ☐ **E** Evaporation gets slower as the liquid gets hotter.
- ☐ **F** Liquids *only* evaporate at temperatures below their melting point.

5 Draw *one* line from each change to show whether it is a physical or chemical change.

Change   **Type of change**

boiling a kettle to make steam

mixing sand and water   chemical change

frying an egg

iron rails rusting   physical change

water turning to ice

7Ha SORTING RESOURCE DATA (WS)

1 Complete the sentences using words from the box. Use each word once.

data	descriptions	discrete	limited	numbers	quantitative

.... data uses numbers. Qualitative data uses ....

Quantitative data can be continuous or .... Continuous data can have any value between two .... Discrete .... has a .... number of choices.

2a The scatter graph shows the relationship between two variables that are both quantitative. Write a set of rules for drawing a good scatter graph.

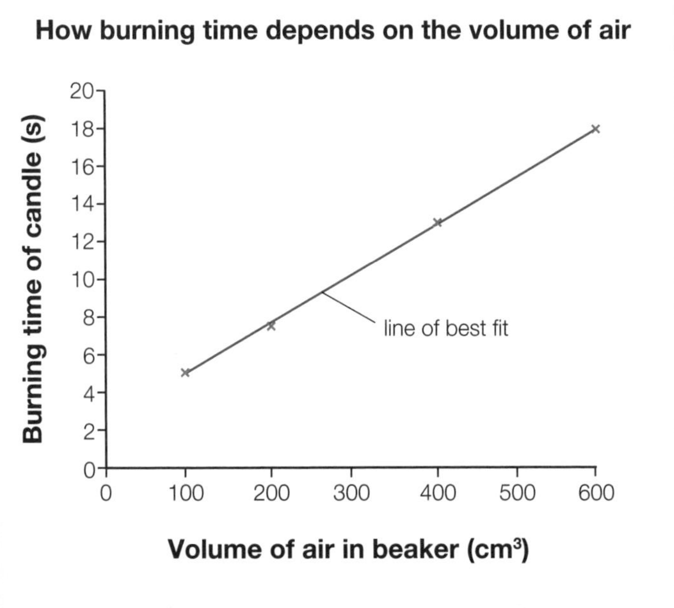

How burning time depends on the volume of air
Burning time of candle (s)
0
2
4
6
8
10
12
14
16
18
20
line of best fit
0
100
200
300
400
500
600
Volume of air in beaker (cm³)

....

....

....

....

....

....

....

b Work in a group to share ideas by comparing your lists. Write down *two* things about your list that were good.

....

....

c Write down *one* thing about your list that could be improved.

....

3 The table contains information on how long certain metal resources will last if we keep using them at the current rate.

Metal	Years left
nickel	90
copper	61
silver	29
zinc	46

a How could you sort this data in the table?

b Draw a bar chart of the data on the grid below.

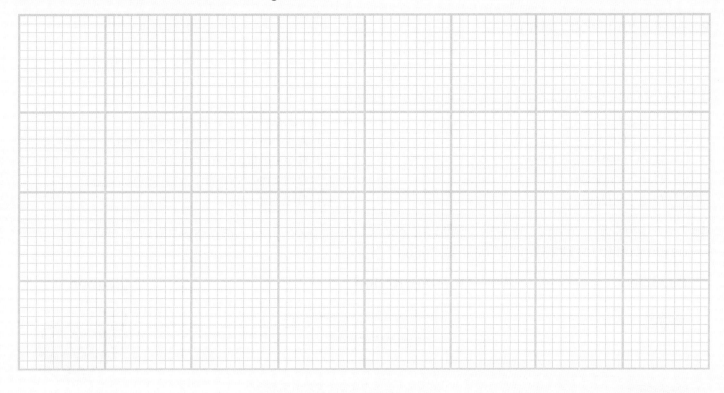

4 The table shows the results of an investigation into how the length of time a candle burns for depends on the volume of air.

a A variable is anything that can change. List the two variables in this experiment.

Volume of air in the beaker (cm³)	Time candle burns for (s)
50	3.9
100	5.2
150	7.1
200	7.6
250	10.6

b **i** Is the data qualitative or quantitative?

ii Is the data continuous or discrete?

7Ha THE AIR WE BREATHE

1 Decide whether each statement is true or false. Cross out the answer you do *not* want.

a Atoms are the simplest particles.	True/False
b Molecules contain only two atoms joined together.	True/False
c The atoms in a molecule must be different.	True/False
d The atoms in a molecule of water can be joined in any way.	True/False

2 What is the periodic table? ....

....

3 Tick (✓) *one* box to answer each of parts **a** and **b** below.

a Pure oxygen is:
  ☐ **A** a mixture.
  ☐ **B** an element.
  ☐ **C** a compound.
  ☐ **D** a solution.

b The reason for this is because:
  ☐ **A** it contains many molecules.
  ☐ **B** it contains many atoms.
  ☐ **C** it only contains one type of atom.
  ☐ **D** it is a gas.

4a Draw *one* line from each particle type to the correct description. Then draw one line from each description to the drawing that *best* illustrates it.

Particle	Description	Diagram
atom	contains only atoms of the same type	
element	the simplest type of particle	
molecule	contains atoms of different types, which are chemically joined	
compound	two or more atoms joined together	

b Describe the difference between:

i elements and compounds ....

....

ii atoms and molecules. ....

5 The following are some gases found in the air.

| argon | carbon dioxide | helium | neon | nitrogen | oxygen |

Complete the sentences using words from the box.

a The gas that makes up the highest percentage of air is ....

b The gas in air that supports burning is ....

c The gas in air that is a compound is ....

6 The water of our seas and oceans covers over half the surface of the Earth. Each water particle is formed by joining two atoms of hydrogen to one atom of oxygen. The sea also contains dissolved substances, including sodium chloride (salt) and oxygen gas, which supports all sea life.

Using examples of substances from the above passage explain the difference between pure substances and mixtures, elements and compounds, and atoms and molecules.

....

....

....

....

....

....

....

....

....

1 What is all matter made up of? _____

2 The elements found in the Earth's crust are shown in the pie chart.

Tick (✓) the percentage data shown in the pie chart.

☐ **A** qualitative
☐ **B** discrete
☐ **C** quantitative
☐ **D** descriptive

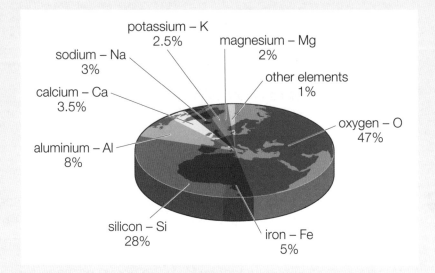

potassium – K
2.5%

magnesium – Mg
2%

sodium – Na
3%

other elements
1%

calcium – Ca
3.5%

oxygen – O
47%

aluminium – Al
8%

silicon – Si
28%

iron – Fe
5%

3 Complete the sentences using words from the box. Use each word once.

atoms	element	joined	molecule	same	two

A compound contains _____ or more elements that are chemically

_____. Gold is an _____ because all the

_____ in gold are the _____ type. Oxygen gas is a

_____ of two oxygen atoms joined together.

4 Give the symbols for the following elements.

a iron _____ **b** sodium _____ **c** calcium _____

5a Which gas from the air do we need to help things burn? _____

b Give the names of *two* gases in the air that are elements.

_____

6 Complete the following sentences.

a A property of gold is that it is shiny. This makes gold useful for _____.

b Copper is a good conductor of heat. This is why copper is used to make _____.

c Carbon, as graphite, is soft. This is why graphite is used to make _____.

B

1 Write down *three* physical properties of most metals.

....

2 Which three metals are magnetic?

....

3 Iodine is a non-metal. It is a dark grey, brittle solid that melts at 114 °C and does not conduct heat or electricity. How is iodine similar to sulfur?

....

4 The properties of elements A and B are compared in the table.

Property	Element A	Element B
melting point	1085 °C	–7 °C
boiling point	2562 °C	59 °C
conductor of heat	yes	no
conductor of electricity	yes	no
malleable	yes	no

a Explain whether element A is a metal or a non-metal.

Element A is a ....

This is because ....

....

b Explain which element would be used to make the wires in a lamp.

....

c Which properties in the table are quantitative data? ....

....

5 Silicon is a non-metal. Describe *one* way in which it is similar to a metal.

....

6 Give *one* reason why we recycle aluminium products.

Recycling aluminium is useful because ....

7Hc OBTAINING METALS (STEM)

1 What is the name given to a rock from which a metal can be obtained? ....

2 Complete the paragraph by crossing out the incorrect term in each sentence.

Crushing rock is a *physical / chemical* process. The ore is then removed and heated to separate the metal from the rest of the compound. In a *physical / chemical* process new substances are made. Changes of state are *physical / chemical* processes.

3 The ore malachite contains copper carbonate.

a Name the elements other than copper present in copper carbonate.

....

b How many of the elements in copper carbonate are metals? ....

4 The following data is about a proposed copper mine.

	Costs per 1000 kg of ore handled
The amount of copper that can be obtained from the ore is 1%. The present selling price of copper is £4.50 per kg.	survey and research = £11.00
	mining operations = £19.50
	transport of ore = £10.00
	extracting metal = £31.00
	admin and sales = £14.00
	distribution of metal = £4.50

a You need to work out if the mine will make a profit or not. Do you have all the data that you will need? Look at diagram A in 7Hc Obtaining Metals to check.

....

....

b Calculate the total cost of handling 1000 kg of the copper ore.

....

....

c Show that the mine is not going to make a profit.

....

....

d What would the selling price need to be to avoid making a loss?

....

7Hd MAKING COMPOUNDS

1 What is the difference between a mineral and an ore?

_____

_____

2 Complete the sentences by crossing out the incorrect terms.

Elements / compounds are made when *elements / compounds* join together. During the reaction, the *elements / compounds* form bonds. The new *element / compound* made has different properties from the *elements / compounds* found in it.

3 Silicon dioxide is a very common substance in the Earth's crust. Tick (✓) the statements that are true.

☐ **A** Silicon dioxide is a mixture of silicon and oxygen.
☐ **B** Silicon dioxide is made from a metal joined with a non-metal.
☐ **C** Silicon dioxide is a compound made from silicon and oxygen.
☐ **D** Silicon dioxide has properties that are the same as those of oxygen.
☐ **E** Silicon dioxide is an element, which is what makes it valuable.
☐ **F** Silicon dioxide is a mixture of compounds.

4 When a compound name ends in *–ide,* the compound contains just two elements. The name of the metal element goes first. Write the names of the compounds formed when the following pairs of elements join.

a potassium and bromine _____

b calcium and oxygen _____

c tin and sulfur _____

d fluorine and magnesium _____

5 Read the following statements then answer the questions below.

Iron reacts with sulfur to form iron sulfide. We need to heat the test tube to get the reaction started, but once going, it will keep glowing and giving out heat.

a circle the non-metal element

b underline the phrase that provides evidence that energy is being given out

c highlight the compound made.

6 When some powdered aluminium is mixed with crystals of iodine, nothing happens. If a few drops of warm water are added, flames and purple fumes are produced and a white solid is left.

a What tells you a reaction has occurred? _____

b What is the name of the compound formed? _____

SB

1 What happens in all chemical reactions?

....

2 List *three* criteria used to decide if a chemical reaction is taking place.

....

....

3 Nitrogen dioxide is formed when oxygen reacts with the most common gas in the air. In this reaction, name the:

a reactant(s) ....

b product(s). ....

4 Write word equations for these reactions.

a magnesium metal burning in oxygen gas to produce magnesium oxide

....

b hydrogen gas combining with iodine to form hydrogen iodide

....

c aluminium iodide being formed when iodine and aluminium react

....

5a Complete these word equations for thermal decomposition reactions.

i mercury oxide → mercury + ...

ii copper carbonate → copper oxide + ...

iii calcium carbonate → .... + carbon dioxide

iv magnesium carbonate → .... + ...

b How is the reaction in **i** different from the reactions in **ii** to **iv**?

....

c What test could we use to identify the gas formed in reaction **iii**?

....

....

6 When potassium permanganate is heated in the apparatus shown below, the following reaction occurs:

potassium permanganate → potassium manganate + manganese dioxide + oxygen

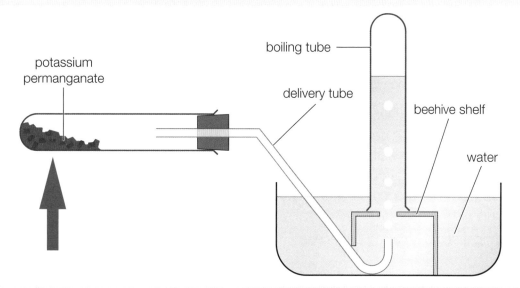

a Explain why this is a chemical reaction.

_____

b What will collect in the boiling tube? _____

c What does the red arrow represent? _____

d Tick (✓) the name of this type of reaction.

   ☐ **A** neutralisation   ☐ **C** oxidation

   ☐ **B** thermal decomposition   ☐ **D** combustion

7 Which statement *best* describes the thermal decomposition of hydrated (blue) copper sulfate?
Tick (✓) *one* box.

   ☐ **A** There is a physical change, forming white copper sulfate and water.

   ☐ **B** The atoms in the copper sulfate break apart to form different atoms, in a chemical reaction.

   ☐ **C** The copper sulfate evaporates.

   ☐ **D** There is a chemical reaction, in which one of the products is water.

8 What elements are in:

a sodium phosphate _____

b lead nitrate _____

c copper sulfate? _____

1 Read the paragraph below.

a Underline all the metal elements in one colour.

b Underline all the non-metal elements in another colour.

c Underline all the compounds in a different colour.

Add your colours to the boxes on the right to act as a key.

Key

Lead is mainly used to make batteries and is produced in many low-income countries. Its ores usually contain minerals such as lead sulfide or lead oxide. Getting pure lead out of these minerals involves several stages, using chemical reactions. The first stages remove impurities (e.g. sulfur) from the minerals. Extremely high temperatures are then used to get the pure lead, and in the process lead dust and smoke are released. The process produces wastes that contain poisonous metals, such as lead, arsenic and mercury.

d State *one* problem caused by making batteries.

....

2 Give three properties that can be used to separate metals and non-metals.

i ....

ii ....

iii ....

3a Which drawing shows a chemical reaction and which shows a change of state?

....

....

....

....

b Give a reason for your answer.

....

....

A eggs frying   **B** water boiling

1 Write down where the energy comes from for Diego to do the following:

a walk to the bus stop _____

b take the bus to school _____

c read a book in bed using a torch. _____

2 Which of the activities in question **1** needed the most energy and which needed the least? How do you know?

Activity that needed the most energy: _____

Activity that needed the least energy: _____

How you know: _____

3 Write down three different ways you use energy:

a at home

i _____

ii _____

iii _____

b at school.

i _____

ii _____

iii _____

4 Write down two different ways energy can be used to cook food.

i _____

ii _____

5 Some cars have batteries that store energy, for an electric motor. The batteries are recharged using mains electricity. Discuss in a group where the energy in the batteries originally comes from. Write your answer below and why your group thinks this.

Where the energy stored in batteries comes from: _____

Why we think this: _____

1 Draw *one* line from each scientific term to its definition.

Scientific term	Definition
balanced diet	all the things you eat
diet	a substance in food that your body needs
nutrient	the unit for measuring energy
joule (J)	a diet that gives you the right amount of energy and all the nutrients you need

SB

2 Why does your body need food?

SB

3 Explain the link between the amount of food someone eats, the amount of activity they carry out and the amount of weight they gain.

4 The table shows the energy contents of some foods.

Food	Energy (kJ/100g)	Portion size (g)	Energy per portion (kJ)
rice, boiled	500	180	900
peas	360	80	
roast lamb	1100	90	
dahl (lentils)	450	150	

a Work in a group to discuss how you will calculate the values to complete the table. Write down your idea and ask your teacher to check it. Then complete the table.

How to calculate the values:

b Manee needs 9000 kJ per day to stay healthy. If each meal contains one portion each of rice, lamb and peas, calculate the number of meals she must eat each day.

FAIR COMPARISONS AND RATIOS (WS)

A student investigates the energy stored in different kinds of biscuit. He does this by burning pieces of each biscuit beneath a boiling tube of water. He measures the temperature rise of the water. The table shows his results.

Biscuit	Mass of biscuit (g)	Temperature rise (°C)	Temperature rise per g (°C)
A	1.2	1.5	
B	3.9	6.0	
C	1.5	1.5	

1 Write down two things the student must keep the same to make this a fair test.

i ....

ii ....

2a Explain how you can calculate the temperature rise per gram for each biscuit.

....

b Calculate the temperature rise per gram and write your answers in the table.

c Explain why we need to calculate the temperature rise per gram to compare different types of biscuit.

....

....

3 What is the ratio of the temperature rises per gram for biscuits A and B?

....

4 The temperature rise per gram of cheese burnt is 4.0 °C, and the temperature rise from burning 1 g of bread is 2.0 °C. A student says 'I would get the same energy from eating 50 g of bread or 25 g of cheese.' Is the student correct? Explain your answer.

....

....

....

5 Peas store 300 kJ of energy in 100 g, oranges store 150 kJ, and carrots store 100 kJ. What is the ratio of the energy stored in peas compared with:

a carrots ....

b oranges? ....

71b ENERGY TRANSFERS AND STORES

1 Use a pencil to tick (✓) *one* box to answer each of these questions.

a How is energy stored in a mug of hot water?
☐ **A** gravitational potential energy
☐ **B** thermal energy
☐ **C** strain energy
☐ **D** kinetic energy

d How is energy stored in a moving car?
☐ **A** gravitational potential energy
☐ **B** thermal energy
☐ **C** strain energy
☐ **D** kinetic energy

b How is energy stored in a box on a high shelf?
☐ **A** gravitational potential energy
☐ **B** thermal energy
☐ **C** strain energy
☐ **D** kinetic energy

e How is energy stored in a bent ruler?
☐ **A** gravitational potential energy
☐ **B** thermal energy
☐ **C** strain energy
☐ **D** kinetic energy

c How is energy stored in a stretched elastic band?
☐ **A** gravitational potential energy
☐ **B** thermal energy
☐ **C** strain energy
☐ **D** kinetic energy

f How is energy stored in water at the top of a waterfall?
☐ **A** gravitational potential energy
☐ **B** thermal energy
☐ **C** strain energy
☐ **D** kinetic energy

2a Ask your teacher to tell you how many of your answers to question **1** were correct.

b Work with others and the Student Book to identify your incorrect answers. Make corrections and check your answers with your teacher. Do this until they are all correct.

SB 3 Diesel fuel is a store of energy in chemical substances. Write down *three* other things that store energy in chemical substances.

_____

4 Uranium is a fuel used in nuclear power stations. What is the name for the way energy is stored in

uranium? _____

5 Use words from the box to complete these sentences. Use each word once.

conservation	created	stored	stores	transferred

Energy can be _____ between different _____.

When this happens it is not used up. Energy can be _____ and transferred

in different ways, but it cannot be _____ or destroyed. This is the law of

_____ of energy.

102

B

6 Write down *three* things that:

a transfer energy by heating or light _____

_____

b transfer energy by sound _____

_____

c use energy transferred by electricity. _____

_____

7 Write down *three* things that use energy transferred by forces. _____

_____

8 A student uses a catapult to launch a toy aeroplane. Complete the flow diagram to show the energy changes.

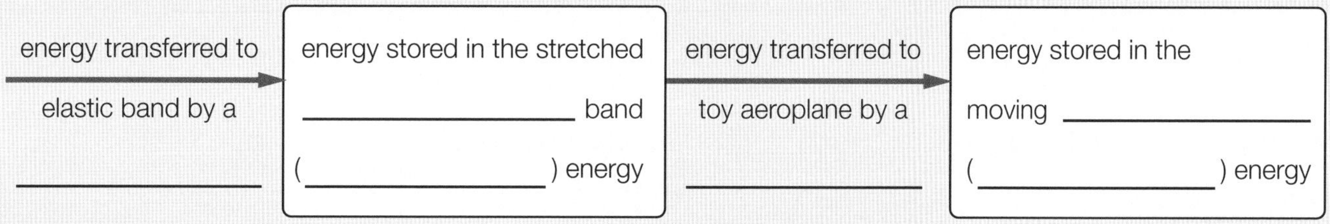

energy transferred to	energy stored in the stretched	energy transferred to	energy stored in the
elastic band by a	_____ band	toy aeroplane by a	moving _____
_____	(_____) energy	_____	(_____) energy

B

9 The flow diagram below shows the energy stores and transfers for a room being heated by an electric fire. The electricity comes from a nuclear power station.

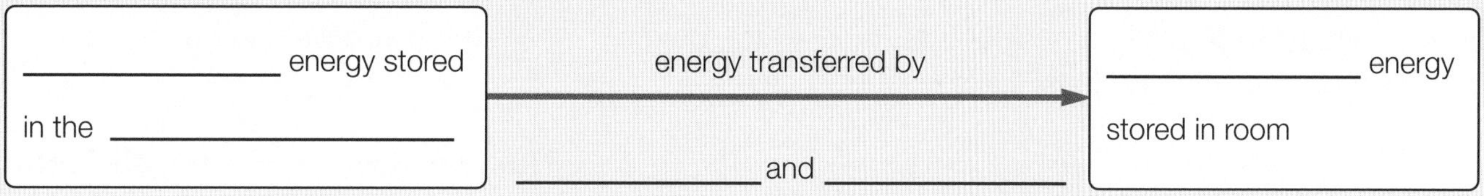

_____ energy stored	energy transferred by	_____ energy
in the _____	_____ and _____	stored in room

a Add the names of the two energy stores (in the squares) and the energy transfers (on the arrow).

b 2000 J of energy goes into the electric fire every second. How much energy is transferred out of it? Explain your answer.

_____

c Draw a similar diagram for a car travelling along a road.

1 How do we obtain the energy stored in fuels such as coal or gas?

....

SB

2 Write down three things humans use fuels for.

i ....

ii ....

iii ....

3a Which fossil fuel is made from the remains of plants? ....

b Why is being buried in mud important when fossil fuels are formed?

....

c How do animal and plant remains get turned into fossil fuels?

....

....

....

d How long does it take for fossil fuels to form? Underline one response.

hundreds of years   thousands of years   millions of years

4 Oil obtained from underground is called crude oil. Name two fuels made from crude oil.

i ....   **ii** ....

5 Uranium is an example of a nuclear fuel. Tick (✓) the boxes to show the similarities and differences between nuclear fuel and fossil fuels.

	Nuclear fuel	Fossil fuels
found underground	☐	☐
made from the remains of living organisms	☐	☐
used in cars and lorries	☐	☐
used to generate electricity	☐	☐

SB

6 A friend of yours says, 'Electricity is a fuel'. Explain why your friend is wrong.

....

....

7 The graph shows scientific estimates for how long supplies of different fossil fuels will last.

a Which fossil fuel will run out first?

_____

b Why do you think the bars on the graph have no definite ends?

_____

_____

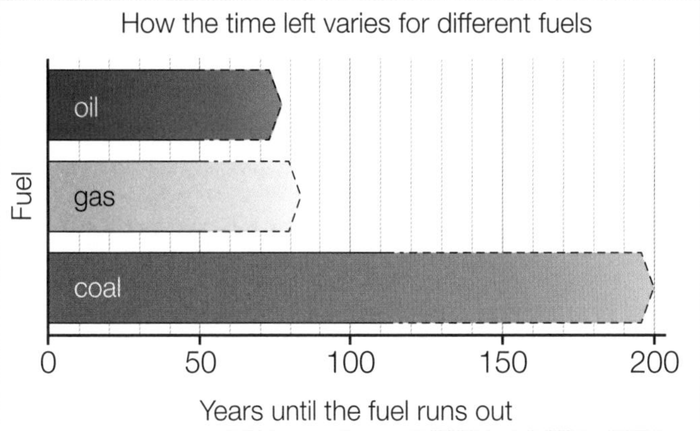

_____

How the time left varies for different fuels

Fuel: oil, gas, coal

0   50   100   150   200

Years until the fuel runs out

8 Fossil fuels are being formed slowly in the Earth today, so why are fossil fuels called non-renewable fuels?

_____

_____

9 What can biofuels be made from? Tick (✓) *two* boxes.
- ☐ waste materials from animals
- ☐ natural gas
- ☐ hydrogen
- ☐ plants
- ☐ crude oil
- ☐ alcohol

10 Use words from the box to complete these sentences. You may use some words more than once.

burnt	electricity	energy	fuel cells	gas
natural gas	non-renewable	oxygen	renewable	water

Hydrogen _____ is used as a fuel. Today, most hydrogen is made from

_____ . Natural gas is a _____ fuel, so the hydrogen

made from it is also _____ .

Scientists are trying to make hydrogen cheaply from _____ . If the

_____ used for this process comes from _____

resources, the hydrogen will be a _____ fuel.

Hydrogen can be _____ to release energy. Hydrogen can also be used in

_____ , which combine hydrogen with _____ from the

air to produce _____ .

1 Lorries used to transport goods need fuel.

a Write down two non-renewable fuels that can be used by lorries.

   i ....   **ii** ....

b How is energy stored in the fuels in part **a**? ....

c Write down a renewable fuel that can be used by lorries. ....

2 The Voyager 1 spacecraft is the furthest human-made object from the Sun. It is over 20 billion km away. Discuss these questions in a group.

a Suggest what factors the engineers had to take into account when deciding on a power source.

....

b Voyager 1 uses nuclear fuel. Suggest why the engineers chose this.

....

SB

3 Lorries can run on fuels including petrol, hydrogen, and biofuel. Fuels release their energy when they burn. You could investigate the amount of energy released by each fuel by:

- carrying out your own experiment to obtain primary data
- using the results of other people's experiments (secondary data).

Write down *one* advantage and *one* disadvantage for each approach.

Primary data: ....

....

Secondary data: ....

....

SB

4 The map shows five different locations (A to E), and the distance between them in kilometres. Work out the shortest route from A to D.

....

....

1a What are most renewable resources used for? ....

b Write down two renewable resources that can be used directly for heating water.

i .... **ii** ....

2 Complete these sentences to describe *two* different ways in which solar power can be used to generate electricity.

a Solar cells ....

....

b Solar power stations (that do not use cells) ....

....

3 Write down three examples of using water to generate electricity.

i .... **ii** .... **iii** ....

4 Most renewable resources are not available all of the time.

a Use a pencil to tick (✓) the boxes to show when the different resources are available.

Resource	Depends on the weather	Available at any time	Only at certain times of day or night
biofuels	☐	☐	☐
geothermal	☐	☐	☐
hydroelectric	☐	☐	☐
solar	☐	☐	☐
tides	☐	☐	☐
waves	☐	☐	☐
wind	☐	☐	☐

b Work with others and the Student Book to identify your incorrect answers. Make corrections and check your answers with your teacher. Do this until they are all correct.

5 Bunsen burners use energy stored in natural gas. Explain where this energy came from originally, and how it came to be stored in the gas.

....

7Ie USING RESOURCES

1 There are advantages and disadvantages to the renewable and non-renewable energy resources that we use.

a For each statement in the first column of the table, decide whether it describes an advantage or a disadvantage. Complete the next column, writing A (for advantage) or D (for disadvantage).

b Tick (✓) the other boxes to show which statements apply to each type of fuel.

Statement	A or D?	Fossil fuels	Nuclear fuel	Renewable resources
available at any time				
cheaper than other resources				
convenient to use in vehicles				
most are not available all the time				
no polluting gases				
non-renewable				
release polluting gases				
renewable				
very expensive				

2a What is the main gas produced when fossil fuels burn?

b What does this gas do in the atmosphere?

3a Describe three ways in which we could use less fossil fuel.

i

ii

iii

b Give two reasons why it is important to use less fossil fuel.

i

ii

1 A roller coaster ride uses an electric motor to pull the carriages up the track.

a Fill in the gaps in the diagram to show the energy transfers and energy stores.

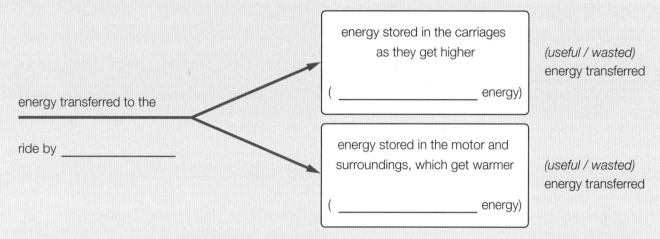

energy stored in the carriages as they get higher

(_____ energy)

(useful / wasted) energy transferred

energy transferred to the

ride by _____

energy stored in the motor and surroundings, which get warmer

(_____ energy)

(useful / wasted) energy transferred

b Cross out the incorrect words in the labels to show which energy store is useful, and which energy store is wasted energy.

2 Two light bulbs receive 20 J of energy every second. Bulb A transfers 18 J by light every second, and bulb B transfers 4 J by light every second. Which bulb is the most efficient? Explain why.

....

....

3 Light bulbs get warm when they are switched on. How much wasted energy is transferred by bulb B every second?

....

4 You are going to complete the diagram below for using a kettle to boil water.

a On a separate piece of paper, write down the words you want to include.

b Share your ideas with a partner or group.
Discuss why you have chosen these words and where they would go.

c Finalise your ideas, and complete the diagram.

7Ie MAKING CHANGES

SB **1** Why do you think that most of the electricity we use in the world is generated from non-renewable resources? Give as many reasons as you can.

....

....

....

....

2 Give two reasons why we need to burn less fossil fuel.

i ....

ii ....

SB **3** Look at the speech bubble. In what way is the person:

a correct

> I always use efficient appliances because they use up less of our country's store of electricity.

....

b wrong? ....

....

4a Some cars have batteries that store energy, which is needed for an electric motor. The batteries have to be recharged using mains electricity. Discuss in a group where the energy in the batteries has originally come from. Write your answer below and why your group thinks this.

Where the energy stored in batteries comes from: ....

Why we think this: ....

b Look back at your answers to this question on page 99. How has your thinking about energy stores and transfers changed now you have studied this unit?

....

....

....

1 Write down three things you will do today that depend on electricity.

i ....

ii ....

iii ....

2 Tick (✓) boxes to show whether each material is a conductor or an insulator.

Material	Conductor	Insulator
plastic	☐	☐
copper	☐	☐
aluminium	☐	☐
rubber	☐	☐
wood	☐	☐
glass	☐	☐

3 The wires used in electrical circuits are made of metal, with a coating of plastic on the outside. Explain why these materials are used.

....

....

....

....

4 A circuit has two cells, a bulb and an open switch, all connected in one loop of wire. Use standard symbols to draw a diagram of the circuit.

7Ja SWITCHES AND CURRENT

1 Draw *one* line from each scientific term to its definition.

Scientific term

ammeter

ampere (A)

component

current

energy

filament

Definition

the unit for measuring current

something that is needed to make things happen or change

a thin piece of wire inside a bulb that glows when current flows through it

something in a circuit, such as a cell or bulb

a component that measures how much electricity is flowing

the flow of electricity around a circuit

2 Explain how a switch works to turn a circuit on and off.

....

....

3a You have a circuit with a cell, a switch and two bulbs. The bulbs light up when you press the switch.

Explain what will happen if you take one of the bulbs out of its holder and then press the switch.

....

....

b Complete the face to show your confidence in your answer – the bigger the smile, the more confident you are.

4 Which statements about current are correct? Tick (✓) *two* boxes.
- ☐ **A** The current is the same everywhere in a circuit.
- ☐ **B** Current is measured using a voltmeter.
- ☐ **C** In a bulb, current flows through a thick piece of wire called the filament.
- ☐ **D** Current only flows if there is a complete circuit.
- ☐ **E** Current needs a switch in order to flow.

5 Circuit X has three bulbs. Circuit Y has four bulbs. They both have one cell. In which circuit will the bulbs

be brighter? ....

6 A torch is not working. Write down all the things that could be wrong with it.

....

1 Complete these sentences using words from the box. Use each word once.

complicated	model	represent	science

There are many different types of _____. All models show or

_____ something. We use models in _____ to help us

to think about _____ things.

2 Write the letters on the drawing of Sam's model to show what each part of the model represents.

X – cell

Y – current

Z – bulb or motor

3 The second drawing shows Nat's model.
Which part (or parts) of the model represent:

a the current _____

b the cell _____

c a bulb or motor? _____

4 Describe what happens to the size of the 'current' as it goes around:

a in Sam's model _____

_____

_____

_____

b in Nat's model. _____

_____

_____

Sam's model

water wheel

The funnel catches all of the water.

pump

water with ink in it

Nat's model

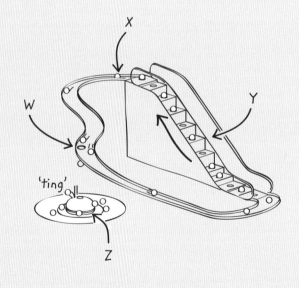

X

W

Y

'ting'

Z

1 Look at Sam's and Nat's circuit models on page 113.

Sam and Nat carry out an investigation to find out which model is better. Which investigation should they do? Tick (✓) *one* box.

- ☐ **A** Set up a circuit with a bulb, and measure the current flowing into the bulb.
- ☐ **B** Measure the current at different places in a circuit.
- ☐ **C** Make circuits with different numbers of cells in the circuit.

SB

2 Predict the results that Sam and Nat should get in their investigation:

a if Sam's model is the better one.

b if Nat's model is the better one.

SB

3 Use what you know about current in circuits to explain which model is better.

4 Explain why Sam and Nat's models are physical models.

5 On the drawing, the arrows represent the different forces on a skydiver.

a Explain why this is an abstract model.

b Describe one other example of an abstract model.

6 Share your answers to questions **4** and **5** with others. Discuss how you can improve your answers. Work together to write a short paragraph to describe the difference between a physical model and an abstract model.

7Jb MODELS FOR CIRCUITS

1 Complete these sentences using words from the box. Use each word once.

charges	components	conducting	current	energy	insulating

A _____ is a flow of tiny _____ in a

wire. The current carries _____ from the cells or power pack to

other _____ in the circuit. Charges can move around easily in

_____ materials like metals. The charges cannot move around in

_____ materials such as plastic.

2 Why do we need to use models to help us to think about electricity?

_____

3 Write the correct number next to each of these statements to
match them to places on the diagram.

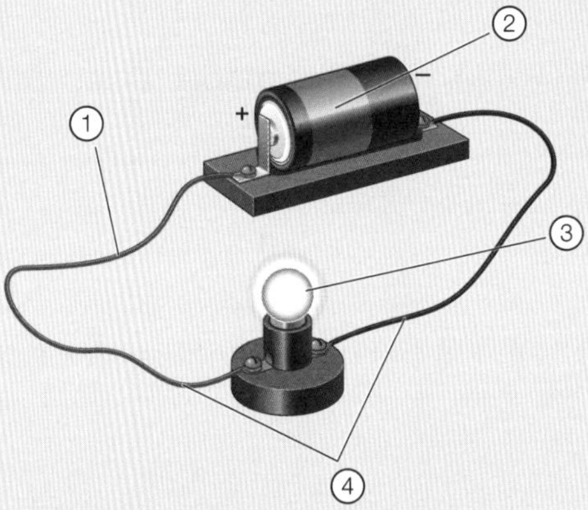

☐ Energy is transferred by light and heating.

☐ The wires let charges flow through them.

☐ All the charges stay in the wires, so the current is the same on
both sides of the bulb.

☐ The cell transfers energy to the charges and pushes them
through the wires.

4 The diagram below shows a central heating system, used in cold countries to keep
homes warm. Which part of the model corresponds to these parts of a circuit?

a bulb _____   **b** wires _____   **c** cell _____

5a What is the same about the water flowing at points X and Y in the diagram?

_____

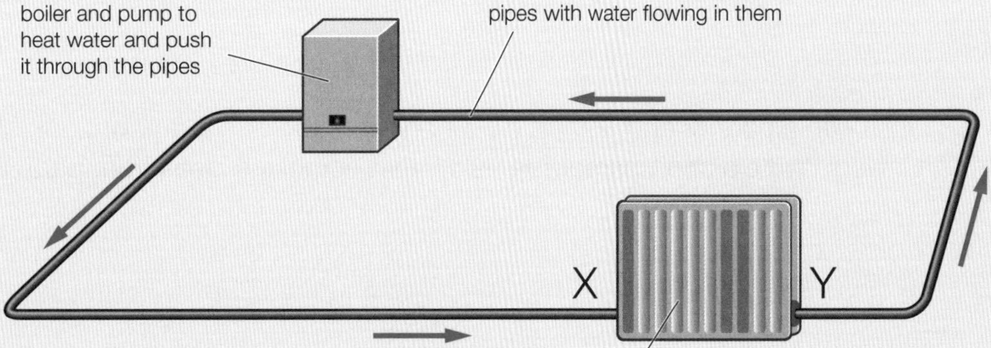

boiler and pump to
heat water and push
it through the pipes

pipes with water flowing in them

b What is different?

_____

radiator to transfer energy
to the room by heating

X   Y

This is a model for helping you to think about electricity.

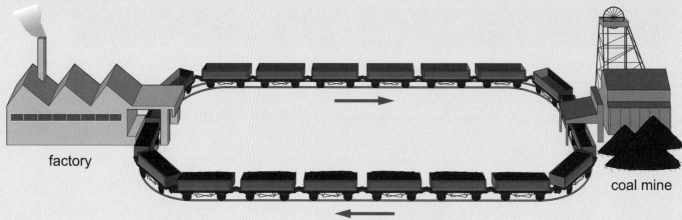

factory

coal mine

SB

1 Look at the drawing. What do you think these things represent?

a the coal mine _____   **c** the train _____

b the factory _____   **d** the coal _____

2 Explain how the model represents the fact that the current is the same everywhere in a circuit.

_____

_____

_____

SB

3 How is the model *not* like an electric circuit?

_____

_____

_____

4a Explain how you could modify the model to add a 'switch' to the 'circuit'.

_____

b How is this different from the way a switch works in a real circuit?

_____

c Work with a partner and compare your answers to parts **a** and **b**. Look for ways to improve your answers. Write a short paragraph below that combines ideas from parts **a** and **b**.

_____

_____

1a In box A, draw a series circuit with one cell and two bulbs.

b In box B, draw a parallel circuit with one cell and two bulbs.

A Series circuit	B Parallel circuit

2 The table shows a 'confidence grid'.
Tick (✓) *one* box for each statement in the table.

Statement	Definitely correct	Might be correct	Might be wrong	Definitely wrong
a The lights in a house are on a series circuit.				
b The current in a series circuit is the same everywhere.				
c All the bulbs in a parallel circuit go out if one of the bulbs breaks.				
d If you add more bulbs to a series circuit, the bulbs do not glow as brightly.				
e If you add more bulbs to a parallel circuit, the current through the cell stays the same.				

3a Does the diagram show an AND or an OR circuit?

....

b Explain your answer. ....

....

4 Complete the table to show what happens in the circuit in question **3**.

5 Amaal says: 'If you want all four bulbs in a circuit to be switched on or off at once, the only way is to use a series circuit.'

Explain why Amaal is wrong. Use a diagram to illustrate your answer.

Switch Y	Switch Z	Bulb
open	open	
closed	open	
open	closed	
closed	closed	

....

....

....

SB

1a What does a voltmeter measure? _____

b Describe the difference between the ways ammeters and voltmeters are put into circuits.

_____

2 Complete this sentence, using the word *energy* in your answer.

The voltage across a component is a way of measuring _____

_____.

3a What does a resistor do in a circuit? _____

_____

b Draw the symbols for a resistor and a variable resistor in the boxes on the right.

SB

4 What happens to the current in a circuit if the resistance of the components in the circuit is increased?

resistor	variable resistor

5 Look at circuits X and Y.

a Explain whether the current in one circuit will be higher than in the other. To answer this, tick (✓) *one* answer for each of parts **a** and **b** below.

☐ **A** X is higher than Y.
☐ **B** Y is higher than X.
☐ **C** Both are the same.
☐ **D** Neither have a current.

b This is because:
☐ **A** the resistance is lower in the series circuit.
☐ **B** the resistance is higher in the parallel circuit.
☐ **C** it is easier for current to flow when there are more branches.
☐ **D** it is more difficult for current to flow when there is more than one way for it to go.

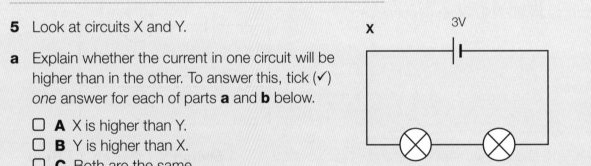
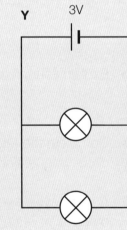

6a Explain what happens to the current in circuit X when you add another bulb in series.

_____

b Explain what happens to the current in circuit Y when you add another bulb in parallel.

1 A self-driving car uses a variable resistor to control the current going to the motor.

a If the current increases, will the car go faster or slower? Explain your answer.

b Explain how the resistance of the variable resistor should be changed to make the car go faster.

c Do the wires connecting the battery to the motor have a high or low resistance? Explain your answer.

2 This is a model for how a human driver controls a car.

Explain whether it is a physical model or an abstract model.

1 Sees an obstacle ahead
↓
2 Decides to slow
↓
3 Presses brake pedal

3 Look at the flowchart.

a Which parts of a human carry out tasks 1, 2 and 3?

b Suggest what a self-driving car could use to carry out tasks 1 and 2.

4a In your *Robear* activity, which task did your group discuss?

b How did you break your task into parts? Write the parts here.

c Explain your solution for one of the parts.

1 Why is there a greater risk of harm from using mains electricity compared to using cells?

2 The box shows two of the safety rules for reducing the risks of using electricity. Explain two things that could happen if you do not follow rule 1.

> **Safety rules**
> **1** Never push things into sockets.
> **2** Do not plug too many things into one socket.

i

ii

3 When several appliances are plugged into one socket, they are all connected in parallel.

a What happens to the current in a parallel circuit if you add more components?

b Explain what could happen if you do not follow rule 2.

4 How confident are you about teaching the reasons for these safety rules to another class?
Tick (✓) *one* box.
- ☐ **A** I am confident of teaching a class about this.
- ☐ **B** I can contribute to a discussion about this.
- ☐ **C** I would rather work with someone else who knows more about this.

SB

5 The three wires inside a cable have different coloured coatings.

a Complete the table to show the colours and names of the three wires.

Name of wire	Colour of coating

b Suggest why the wires need to have standard colours.

SB

6 What could happen if the current in an appliance was too high?

7a What happens to the wire inside a fuse if the current is too high?

b Why are fuses used in plugs?

8 An electrician can choose from the following fuses. Explain which fuse should be used for an appliance that has a current of 6A.

| 3 A | 5 A | 10 A | 13 A |

....

....

9 Name another device that cuts off the current if it becomes too high.

....

10 Complete these sentences to describe what these parts of a plug do.

a The cable grip ....

b The earth wire ....

c The live pin ....

11 How could you find out how much current can flow through a piece of fuse wire before it melts? Write a plan for your investigation, including the apparatus you will need and a circuit diagram.

Method   **Circuit diagram**

....

....

....

....

....

....

....

12 Work in a group to discuss the plans you have written. Then write down *one* way in which you can make your plan better.

....

....

7Je A WORLD WITHOUT ELECTRICITY

1 Draw a circuit with one cell and one bulb.
Add an ammeter to measure the current through the bulb, and a voltmeter to measure the voltage across it.

2 Describe two different things that affect the size of the current in a circuit.

i ....

ii ....

3 Explain why bulbs in a series circuit become less bright when you add more of them.

....

....

....

4 Explain how to use a voltmeter to discover which component in a series circuit is transferring the most energy.

....

....

....

SB

5 Imagine if parallel circuits had never been invented. Suggest how our use of electricity would be different if all circuits had to be series circuits. Use as many ideas from this unit as you can in your answer.

....

....

....

....

....

1 Draw lines to match each unit with the quantity it is used to measure. Some quantities can link to more than one unit.

Quantity

area

length

force

mass

Unit

newton (N)

centimetre (cm)

gram (g)

metre (m)

centimetre squared (cm²)

2a What is the difference between a contact force and a non-contact force?

_____

_____

b Work in a group to list *three* contact forces and *three* non-contact forces. Write your answers below.

Contact forces: _____

Non-contact forces: _____

Ask your teacher to check your answers. If you got any wrong, agree on a better answer. Keep doing this until you have them all correct.

3 Rock climbers use special shoes to help them to cling onto a rock face. They use ropes to stop them hitting the ground if they fall. Discuss the following questions in a group, then write your answers below.

a Describe all the forces on a climber when she is clinging onto the rock. Say what causes each force and how big the forces are compared to each other.

_____

_____

b The climber falls. Describe the forces on her and her speed as she is falling, and as the rope begins to stop her.

_____

_____

c The rope stops the climber. Describe the forces on her as she is hanging on the rope.

_____

SB

1 Write down three ways in which a force can affect a soccer ball.

i ....

ii ....

iii ....

2 Write down *one* thing that each of these forces can do.

Friction: ....

Upthrust: ....

Gravity: ....

Magnetism: ....

Air resistance: ....

Static electricity: ....

3 Look at the forces listed in question **2**. Write down the *three* forces that are non-contact forces.

....

4 The drawing shows three cars.

a Which car has the greatest force on it?

....

b How can you tell?

....

c Draw an arrow next to car C to show a force that is smaller than the forces on the other two cars.

d What will happen to the cars because of the forces on them?

A

B

C

5 The three cars are moving at the same speed. Draw arrows next to the cars to show the forces needed to make:

a car A stop quickly

b car B speed up

c car C slow down gradually.

A

B

C

6 The drawing below shows an airship. It is travelling at a constant speed.

a Use a pencil to add labelled force arrows to the diagram to show the forces on the airship and what causes them.

b Work as a group. Compare your answers to part **a**. Use the Student Book to help you. Make corrections and check your answers with your teacher. Do this until they are all correct.

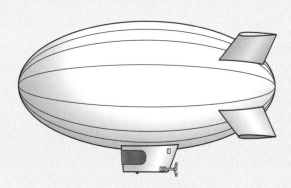

7a What is weight? ....

b What are the units for weight? ....

c What is mass? ....

d What are the units for mass? ....

8 Why would you weigh less on the Moon than you do on the Earth?

....

9a Explain *one* way in which you can change your mass. ....

....

b Explain what happens to your weight when your mass changes.

....

....

1a Which word describes the difference between the original length of an object and its stretched length? Tick (✓) *one* box.

☐ **A** elastic

☐ **B** proportional

☐ **C** extension

☐ **D** plastic

b Which word describes a material that does not return to its original shape when the forces on it are removed? Tick (✓) *one* box.

☐ **A** elastic

☐ **B** proportional

☐ **C** extension

☐ **D** plastic

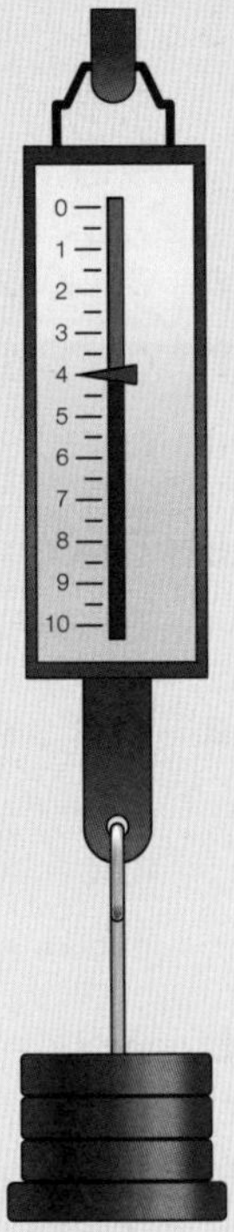

2 Write down the reading on this force meter. _____ unit _____

3 A spring stretches 3 cm when a 5 N weight hangs on it. How far will it stretch with a weight of 15 N?

SB

4 The graph shows how far different materials stretch when a weight is hung on them.

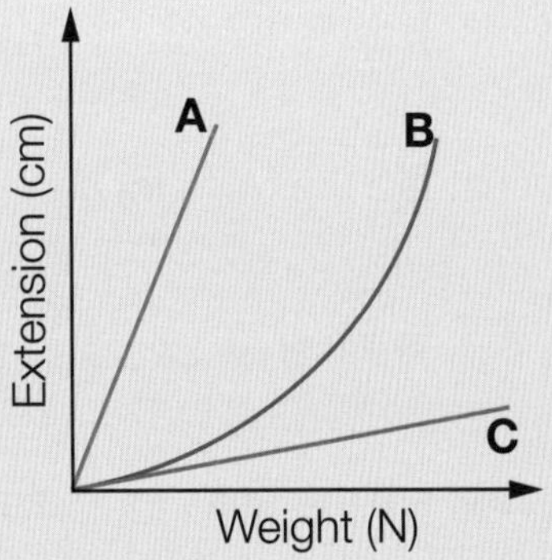

a Which material stretches the most for a certain weight?

b Which material(s) could be used for making a force meter? Explain your reasoning.

c Explain which material would be best for making a force meter to measure small weights.

1 Write H or L next to each material, to show if they have high (H) or low (L) friction.

rubber _____ oil _____ wax _____ sandpaper _____

2 Use words from the box to complete these sentences. Use each word once.

air brakes engines lubricant resistance shapes smooth solid surfaces water

Friction can be useful, such as in car _____. Friction is not useful inside car

_____. We can reduce friction between _____ objects

by making the surfaces _____ or by using a _____.

Friction can be caused by gases (_____ resistance) and by liquids

(_____ resistance). Objects with smooth _____ and

smooth _____ have lower air and water _____.

3a Explain why you should oil the axles of a bicycle. _____

_____

b Explain why you must never put oil on the brake blocks of a bicycle.

_____

c Explain why bicycle brakes do not work well in the rain.

_____

4 Tick (✓) the boxes to show whether each statement is true or false.

Statement	True	False
Friction in a car's brakes is useful.	☐	☐
Tyres grip the road better when it rains.	☐	☐
Lubricating a bicycle makes it harder to ride.	☐	☐
Air resistance can be reduced by giving vehicles a smooth shape.	☐	☐
An engine will soon stop working if there is no oil in it.	☐	☐
Having very smooth soles on your shoes makes walking easier.	☐	☐

1 Use words from the box to complete these sentences. Use each word as many times as you need to.

> force   area

If you keep the _____ the same:

- for a larger _____ the pressure will be lower

- for a smaller _____ the pressure will be higher.

If you keep the _____ the same:

- for a larger _____ the pressure will be higher

- for a smaller _____ the pressure will be lower.

2 Write down the unit for pressure. Unit _____ symbol _____

SB

3a Explain why a drawing pin is easier to push into the wall if the point is sharp.

....

....

b Explain why the drawing pin has a large head for you to push on.

....

....

4 The table shows the weights of some boxes, and the area of each one in contact with the floor.

Box	Weight (N)	Area	Pressure	Units
A	6	$1.5\,cm^2$		
B	9000	$3\,m^2$		
C	6	$20\,cm^2$		
D	200	$0.5\,m^2$		

Work in a group to discuss how you will calculate the values to complete the table. Write down your idea and ask your teacher to check it. Then complete the table.

How to calculate the values: ....

1 Tick (✓) the boxes to show which units are part of the SI system (standard units).

Unit	Standard unit	Not a standard unit
pascal	☐	☐
hour	☐	☐
newton	☐	☐
metre	☐	☐
litre	☐	☐
gram	☐	☐
joule	☐	☐

2 Draw *one* line to match each unit with its symbol and *one* line from the symbol to the quantity it measures.

Unit	Symbol	Quantity
joule	m/s	volume
metre	s	speed
second	m³	time
metre squared	m²	length
kilogram	kg	energy
metre cubed	J	area
metres per second	m	mass

3 Which unit would you use for the following measurements? Choose your answers from question **1**.

a The distance across the playground. _____

b The amount of ground that a soccer pitch covers. _____

c How long it takes you to eat a chocolate. _____

4 Which unit would you use for the following measurements?

a The force on each square metre of ground beneath a concrete block. _____

b The amount of water in a container. _____

c The weight of a bag of flour. _____

d The amount of matter in a bar of gold. _____

7Kd SI UNITS AND PREFIXES (WS)

1 The word box shows the prefixes used with SI units.

| centi- | deci- | kilo- | mega- | micro- | milli- | nano- |

a Why do we use prefixes with SI units? _____

b Use a pencil to write the prefixes in the table in order of size, starting with the smallest. Complete the other columns without looking at the Student Book.

c Work with others and the Student Book to identify your incorrect answers. Make corrections and check your answers with your teacher. Do this until they are all correct.

Prefix	Symbol	Meaning
	n	
micro-		
		$\frac{1}{1000}$
	c	
	d	
		1000
mega-		

2 Which unit would you use for the following measurements? Give the best prefix as well as the unit.

a The length of your thumbnail. _____

b The energy stored in a bag of rice. _____

c The mass of a grain of rice. _____

d The width of a human cheek cell. _____

SB

3a Explain why it is important that all scientists use the same set of units.

_____

_____

b People in different countries use different units of mass or length when buying food or other goods. Explain why this does not usually cause problems.

_____

_____

1a What do unbalanced forces do to a:

i stationary object ....

ii moving object? ....

b What do balanced forces do to a:

i stationary object ....

ii moving object? ....

2 The drawings show a child on a bicycle. Complete the sentences by crossing out the incorrect words.

The forces are *(balanced / unbalanced)*, because the forwards force is *(bigger than / smaller than / the same size as)* the backwards force. The bicycle will *(slow down / speed up / stay at the same speed)*.

The forces are *(balanced / unbalanced)*, because the forwards force is *(bigger than / smaller than / the same size as)* the backwards force. The bicycle will *(slow down / speed up / stay at the same speed)*.

The forces are *(balanced / unbalanced)*, because there is only a *(forwards / backwards)* force. The bicycle will *(slow down / speed up / stay at the same speed)*.

3 Look at the drawings in question **2**.

a How could the child increase the size of the friction forces on the bike?

....

b How would increasing the size of this force affect their speed?

....

4 A girl is riding a bicycle. She starts pedalling as hard as she can. The statements below explain what happens to the bicycle until the girl reaches top speed.

a Work in a group to decide on the order of the statements. Use a pencil to write numbers next to the statements to put them in the correct order.

	As the bicycle speeds up, the friction and air resistance forces get bigger and bigger.
	Eventually they balance the force from the pedals.
	The bicycle goes faster.
	The bicycle is not moving to start with, so the force from the pedals is much greater than friction forces.
	The bicycle starts to move.
	The force from the pedals is still greater than the friction forces.
	This is the top speed of the bicycle.
	When the bicycle is moving slowly, the friction forces are not very big.
	When this happens the bicycle will continue to move at the same speed.

b Work with others and the Student Book to check your answers. Make corrections and check your answers with your teacher. Do this until they are all correct.

5 The girl in question **4** oils her bicycle. Explain how this will affect:

a the friction forces on the bicycle

b her top speed.

6 When you stretch a spring it gets harder and harder to pull it because the spring pulls back. Use this idea to complete the following sentences to explain how a force meter works.

When you first hang something on a force meter

As the spring stretches

Eventually the forces

SB **7** Explain what will happen if a larger mass is put on the force meter in question **6**.

1 One thing that must be agreed is which measurement units to use for a project (e.g. metres, feet, pounds, kilograms). By convention each measurement unit has an internationally agreed symbol.

a Explain why it is important to decide what measurement unit to use.

b Explain why having a convention for unit symbols is important.

2 The diagram shows a car on a bridge.

a Draw a force arrow to show the weight of the car.

b The bridge is not moving. What does this tell you about the size of all the upwards forces compared to the weight of the car?

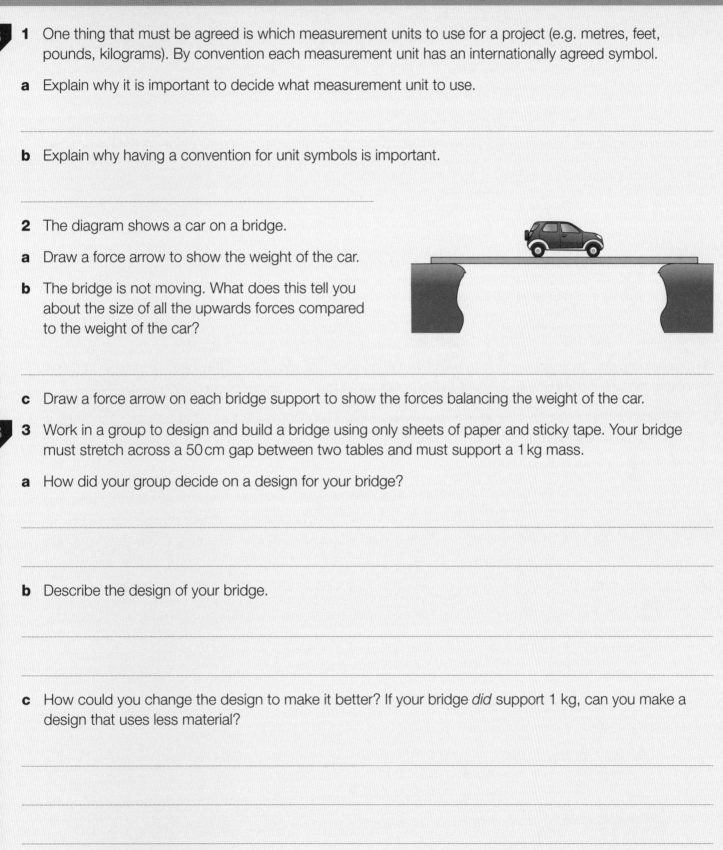

c Draw a force arrow on each bridge support to show the forces balancing the weight of the car.

3 Work in a group to design and build a bridge using only sheets of paper and sticky tape. Your bridge must stretch across a 50 cm gap between two tables and must support a 1 kg mass.

a How did your group decide on a design for your bridge?

b Describe the design of your bridge.

c How could you change the design to make it better? If your bridge *did* support 1 kg, can you make a design that uses less material?

1 Describe the difference between weight and mass, including the units used for measuring them.

_____

_____

SB

2a Skis are available in different sizes. Explain why a person might want to buy a bigger pair of skis. Use ideas about pressure in your answer.

_____

_____

_____

b Describe a situation where high pressure is useful in sports.

_____

_____

3 Rock climbers use special shoes to help them to cling onto a rock face. They use ropes to stop them hitting the ground if they fall. Discuss the questions in a group, then write your answers below.

a Describe all the forces on a climber when she is clinging onto the rock. Say what causes each force and how big the forces are compared to each other.

_____

_____

_____

_____

b The climber falls. Describe the forces on her and her speed as she is falling, and as the rope begins to stop her.

_____

_____

_____

_____

c Look back at your answers to this question on page 123. How has your thinking about forces and their effects changed now you have studied this unit?

_____

_____

7La ANIMAL SOUNDS

1 Write down *two* ways that humans use sounds:

a for communication ....

b for warning. ....

2 Write down *two* different ways that you can make sound with your body.

....

3 What is vibrating when these things make a sound?

a a drum ....

b a guitar ....

c your voice ....

d a recorder or flute ....

e a loudspeaker ....

f a hummingbird ....

4 You make a noise by banging a drum. How will the sound change if you:

a hit the drum harder ....

b use a smaller drum? ....

5 Bats make noises to avoid obstacles and find their prey. Discuss the questions in a group, then write your answers below. (You are not expected to know full answers to these questions.)

a The noises travel as waves. Describe these waves in as much detail as you can.

....

....

....

b Explain how bats can tell how far away an obstacle is using these noises.

....

....

7La MAKING SOUNDS

1 Use a pencil to tick (✓) *one* box to answer each of the following questions.

a Sounds with a high intensity are said to have a:
- ☐ **A** high pitch.
- ☐ **B** high volume.
- ☐ **C** low pitch.
- ☐ **D** low volume.

b The volume of a note depends on:
- ☐ **A** the frequency of the vibrations.
- ☐ **B** the pitch of the sound.
- ☐ **C** the amplitude of the vibrations.
- ☐ **D** the number of vibrations per second.

c The frequency of a note is
- ☐ **A** the number of vibrations per second.
- ☐ **B** the size of the vibrations.
- ☐ **C** the size of the vibrating object.
- ☐ **D** the pitch of the sound.

d You can make a low, quiet sound on tubular bells by:
- ☐ **A** hitting a long bell hard.
- ☐ **B** hitting a short bell hard.
- ☐ **C** hitting a long bell gently.
- ☐ **D** hitting a short bell gently.

2 Ask your teacher how many of your answers to question **1** are correct. Then work with others and the Student Book to identify your incorrect answers. Make corrections and check with your teacher. Do this until they are all correct.

SB

3 A tuning fork vibrates 500 times per second.

a What is its frequency? _____

b How will it sound different from a tuning fork that vibrates 300 times per second?

SB

4 Two male gorillas are beating their chests.

a One makes a lower sound than the other. Suggest what this could tell you about the two gorillas. Explain your answer.

b Explain how one of them can make a louder beating sound than the other.

5 Felipe says 'Large animals always make louder sounds than small animals.' Explain how you could find out if he is right.

7Lb MOVING SOUNDS

1 The diagram shows two sound waves coming from a loudspeaker.

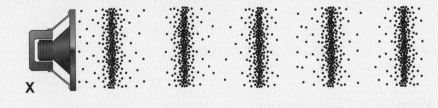

a Draw a labelled arrow ⟶ on one of the sound waves to show the direction in which energy is being transferred.

b Draw a labelled arrow ⟷ on one of the sound waves to show which way the particles move as the wave passes.

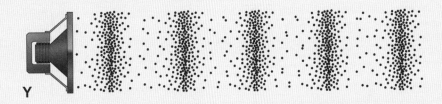

2 Look at the sound waves in the diagram in question **1**.

Which shows the louder sound? Explain your answer. ....

....

3 Two astronauts working outside the International Space Station need to use radios to talk to each other.

a Explain why they need a radio. ....

....

b Astronauts can talk to each other in space without using a radio if they touch their helmets together.

Explain why this works. ....

....

....

c With a partner, compare what you have written for parts **a** and **b**. Look for ways to improve your answer to part **b**. Write an improved answer below.

....

....

....

1 The table shows the speed of sound in some different materials. Draw a bar chart to show this information on the axes provided. Arrange the bars in order of size, label the axes and add a title.

Material	Speed of sound (m/s)
air	343
glass	3950
steel	6100
water	1450
wood	3600

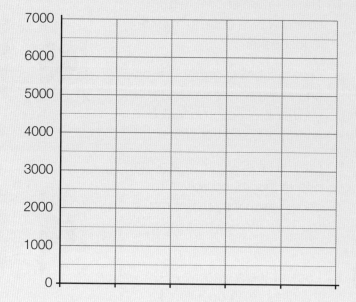

SB

2 Why does sound travel faster in steel than it does in air? Use ideas about particles in your answer.

_____

_____

_____

3 A man is shouting.

a Explain why he sounds quieter as you walk away from him.

_____

_____

b Compare your answer to part **a** with a partner. Use the Student Book to help you write a better answer below.

_____

_____

SB

4 You can make your voice carry further by cupping your hands around your mouth or by shouting through a paper cone. Explain why this works.

_____

_____

SB

1 Look at the table on page 138. Which column of the table shows quantitative data?

---

2 These statements are about line graphs and scatter graphs.

a Use a pencil to tick (✓) the correct boxes to show which kind of graph the statement applies to.

	Line graph	Scatter graph	Neither	
i usually used to show how one variable changes with time	☐	☐	☐	😊
ii a quantitative variable is plotted against a qualitative variable	☐	☐	☐	😊
iii points are joined with a line of best fit	☐	☐	☐	😊
iv used to look for relationships between quantitative variables	☐	☐	☐	😊

b Complete the faces to show how confident you are about each answer.

3 We can use a graph to represent the movement of air particles in a sound wave. The diagrams represent two different sound waves.

A 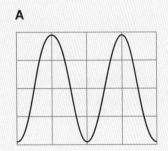 B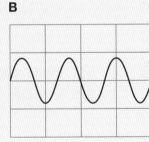

a Which graph shows:

i particles moving only a little way as the wave passes _____

ii the wave with the greater number of waves per second? _____

b Complete these sentences by crossing out the incorrect words.

Wave A has the *(highest / lowest)* frequency. It will make a *(higher / lower)* note than wave B.

Wave A has the *(largest / smallest)* amplitude. It will be *(louder / quieter)* than wave B.

The graph shows how the speed of sound depends on the temperature of the air.

SB

1 Describe what the graph tells us about the speed of sound in air.

....

....

....

....

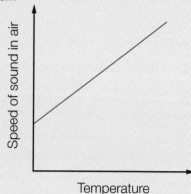

2 Relative humidity is a measure of the amount of water vapour in the air.

Aisha says that the speed of sound in water will decrease when there are more water molecules in the air.

a The table shows the speed of sound at different relative humidities. Plot the data on the axes below. Join the points with a line of best fit, label the axes and add a title.

b Describe the shape of the graph.

....

....

c Is Aisha correct? Explain your answer. ....

....

Relative humidity (%)	Speed of sound (m/s)
0	387
10	392
20	398
30	404
40	410
50	415
60	421
70	427
80	432
90	437
100	443

d Complete the face to show how well you think you have drawn the graph – a big smile means you think you have done it well.

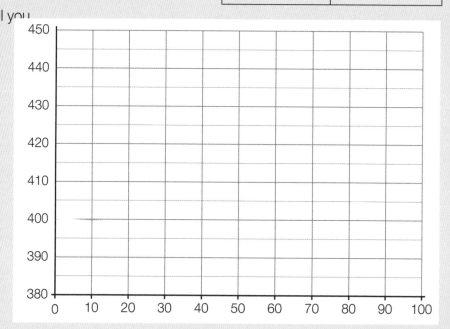

SB **1** Write down the parts of the ear in order, starting with the one that vibrates first when a sound wave arrives: bones, cochlea, eardrum.

....

2 The statements describe different parts of the ear. Write the correct name next to each part, using words from the box. You will need to use some words more than once.

| auditory | nerve | bones | cochlea | ear | canal | eardrum |

a amplify vibrations ....

b detects vibrations in a liquid and sends impulses ....

c vibrates when sound waves reach it ....

d a thin membrane ....

e sends nerve impulses to the brain ....

f channels sound waves to the ear drum ....

SB **3** In some countries, employers must provide hearing protection if the noise level is above 85 dB.

Why is this necessary? ....

....

SB **4** How could you find out which materials are the best sound insulators? Write a plan for an investigation.

....

....

....

....

....

5 Share your answer to question **4** with others. Discuss how well you have explained your method, how your test is fair, and how you will decide which materials are the best. Write down *one* thing that you could improve about your plan.

....

....

1a Describe how a microphone works. Your answer should include the words in the box.

changes	current	diaphragm	vibrations

....

....

....

b Share your answer to part **a** with others. Discuss your answer, and use the Student Book to help you to improve it. Write your improved answer below.

....

....

....

2 Explain the difference between infrasound and ultrasound.

....

....

....

3 The diagram shows the range of frequencies that some animals can hear.

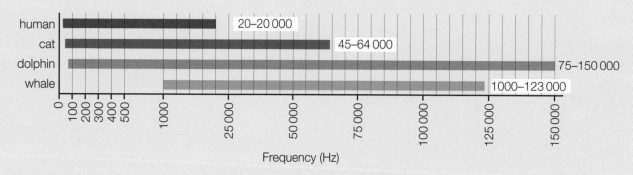

Frequency (Hz)

a Which of the animals in the chart has the greatest hearing range? ....

b Which animal can hear the lowest frequency? ....

SB 4 Cats have similar structures in their ears to humans. Describe how a cat hears.

....

....

7Ld USING SOUND

1 These scientific terms describe different things when a sound wave transfers energy to a material. Draw *one* line from each term to its definition.

Scientific term	Definition
absorb	the energy bounces off the material
transmit	the energy passes through the material
reflect	the energy stays inside the material

2a Write down *two* things that bats and dolphins use echolocation for.

....

b Write down *two* things they can work out from the echoes they detect.

....

3 Each bat can produce different frequencies of ultrasound. Explain why this is useful if there are many bats hunting together.

....

4 The diagram shows a ship using sonar to find out how deep the sea is.

a Complete the sentences to write a description for what is happening in each part of the diagram.

In part A, the sonar equipment on the ship ....

....

In B, the ....

In C, the ....

The sonar equipment works out the depth using ....

....

b Explain how the ship can detect that there are fish swimming above the sea bed.

....

c Share your answer to part **b** with a partner. Discuss how you can make it better, and write your improved answer below.

....

The bar chart shows the results of an investigation into noise levels at a school.

1 Why is it useful to present data in bar charts or graphs?

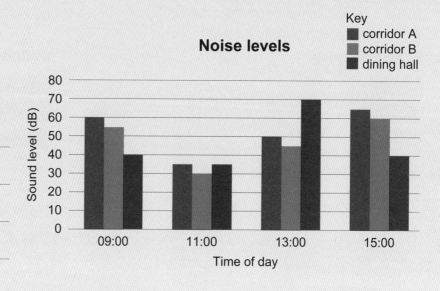

Noise levels

Key
- corridor A
- corridor B
- dining hall

2 Suggest what students in the school are doing at the following times, and give reasons for your answers.

a 11:00

b 13:00

3a Write down *three* different sources of noise in your school.

b How could these unwanted noises be reduced?

4 In the practical task, you used a sound meter app to investigate the noise levels in your school.

a Write a conclusion for your investigation.

b How well did your findings match your predictions?

c Vadim says 'We did our investigation in lesson time. The corridors are always the quietest parts of the school.' Explain why his conclusion is *not* valid.

1 The drawing below shows a wave.

a Label the drawing using words and phrases from the box.

amplitude	crest	direction of travel	particle movement	trough

b Compare your answers to part **a** with a partner to check for mistakes. Mark any corrections to your labels in a different colour.

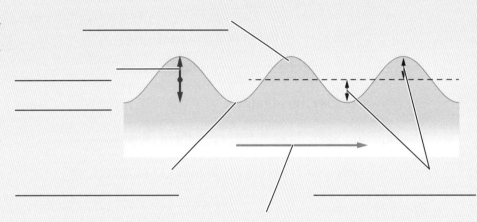

SB **2** Which way will ducks on a pond move as waves pass them?

SB **3** You drop a stone into a pond.

a What happens to some of the energy that was stored in the falling stone?

b How could you make waves on the pond with a larger amplitude?

4 Complete these sentences by crossing out the incorrect words.

The greater the amplitude of a wave, the *(less / more)* energy it is transferring. As waves spread out from a source, the energy they transfer gets more *(concentrated / spread out)* and so the amplitude of the waves gets *(larger / smaller)*.

SB **5** People in small boats need to be careful if they are sailing near cliffs, because the waves can be bigger than in the open sea, and may be coming from more than one direction. Explain why this is.

1 Tuning fork B is tapped harder than A.

a Explain *two* differences in the sounds made by the two tuning forks.

_____

_____

b These statements explain how you hear the sound made by the tuning forks. Write numbers next to them to show the correct order.

☐ The vibrations spread out as longitudinal waves.

☐ Ear bones amplify the vibrations.

☐ The vibrating forks make the air near them vibrate.

☐ In the cochlea, vibrations are converted to nerve impulses.

☐ Some of the waves go down your ear canal and make the ear drum vibrate.

A   B

2 Bats make noises to avoid obstacles and find their prey. Discuss the questions in a group, then write your answers below.

a The noises travel as waves. Describe these waves in as much detail as you can.

_____

_____

_____

b Explain how bats can tell how far away an obstacle is using these noises.

_____

_____

c Look back at your answers to this question on page 135. How has your thinking about sound changed now you have studied this unit?

_____

_____

COMMAND WORDS

Command word	Meaning
Add/label	Add labels to a diagram or add information to a diagram, table, chart or graph (e.g. adding units to a table).
Calculate	Produce a numerical answer. Remember to show your working.
Circle	Identify a point on a graph or diagram by circling it.
Comment on	See 'Evaluate'.
Complete	Add words to a sentence or add information to a table, graph or diagram.
Deduce	Make a conclusion using the information provided.
Define	Give a brief explanation of what something means.
Describe	Say what something or someone is like or give an account of events.
Design	Plan or invent a way of doing something using your scientific knowledge.
Determine	Select and use numbers from the question (and/or graph) to do a calculation.
Discuss	Identify an issue that is being talked about in the question, and then write about the different aspects of the issue (advantages, disadvantages etc.). You may also need to write an argument in support of or against a particular idea.
Draw	Draw a diagram. Remember that some diagrams will need you to use a ruler (e.g. circuit diagrams).
Estimate	Calculate using rounded or approximate values.
Evaluate	Point out the good/bad points about things and use these points to say whether overall you think things are good or bad.
Explain	Give a reason why something is as it is or how it operates. Use words such as *because* to make clear why things happen.
Give	Write down a simple fact or statement. (Same as 'State' and 'Write down'.)
Give a reason	Give reasons why something is a certain way, including why it operates as it does. Use words such as *because* to make clear why things happen.
Identify	Select some information from a table, chart, graph or text.
List	Write down the steps, terms, etc., that are asked for. No description or explanation is needed. Sometimes the steps need to be given in order.
Name	Write down the name of something.
Outline	State the main points of something (e.g. an argument, a process that involves many steps).

COMMAND WORDS

Plot	Mark points accurately on a grid using data that has been given to you. If you have to draw a chart or graph, remember the points below. All charts and graphs need • to fill as much of the paper as possible • axis lines drawn in • divisions on the scales evenly spaced • numbers on the scales written in • axes labelled • units in brackets or with a solidus, after each axis label • a title • to be plotted accurately • to be drawn in (sharp) pencil For scatter and line graphs • to be plotted with small neat crosses • possible line of best fit For bar charts • for discontinuous data leave gaps between the bars • for grouped continuous data there are no gaps
Predict	Describe an expected result. You can often use 'If …, then …' to make a prediction (e.g. if the air hole on the Bunsen burner is opened wider, then the flame will be hotter).
Sketch	Draw a diagram or graph in freehand. A sketched graph needs a line and labelled axes. The axes do not have scales.
State	Write down a simple fact or statement. (Same as 'Give' and 'Write down'.)
Suggest	Use your scientific knowledge to put forward an idea of your own.
Tick	Add a tick (✓) to make a choice.
Use the information	Make use of the data that is given to you in your answer.
Write down	Write down a simple fact or statement. (Same as 'Give' and 'State'.)

Legend:
- metal
- semi-metal
- non-metal

1 H hydrogen																		2 He helium
3 Li lithium	4 Be beryllium											5 B boron	6 C carbon	7 N nitrogen	8 O oxygen	9 F fluorine	10 Ne neon	
11 Na sodium	12 Mg magnesium											13 Al aluminium	14 Si silicon	15 P phosphorus	16 S sulfur	17 Cl chlorine	18 Ar argon	
19 K potassium	20 Ca calcium	21 Sc scandium	22 Ti titanium	23 V vanadium	24 Cr chromium	25 Mn manganese	26 Fe iron	27 Co cobalt	28 Ni nickel	29 Cu copper	30 Zn zinc	31 Ga gallium	32 Ge germanium	33 As arsenic	34 Se selenium	35 Br bromine	36 Kr krypton	
37 Rb rubidium	38 Sr strontium	39 Y yttrium	40 Zr zirconium	41 Nb niobium	42 Mo molybdenum	43 Tc technetium	44 Ru ruthenium	45 Rh rhodium	46 Pd palladium	47 Ag silver	48 Cd cadmium	49 In indium	50 Sn tin	51 Sb antimony	52 Te tellurium	53 I iodine	54 Xe xenon	
55 Cs caesium	56 Ba barium	57 La lanthanum	72 Hf hafnium	73 Ta tantalum	74 W tungsten	75 Re rhenium	76 Os osmium	77 Ir iridium	78 Pt platinum	79 Au gold	80 Hg mercury	81 Tl thallium	82 Pb lead	83 Bi bismuth	84 Po polonium	85 At astatine	86 Rn radon	
87 Fr francium	88 Ra radium	89 Ac actinium	104 Rf rutherfordium	105 Db dubnium	106 Sg seaborgium	107 Bh bohrium	108 Hs hassium	109 Mt meitnerium	110 Ds darmstadtium	111 Rg roentgenium	112 Cn copernicium	113 Nh nihonium	114 Fl flerovium	115 Mc moscovium	116 Lv livermorium	117 Ts tennessine	118 Og oganesson	

58 Ce cerium	59 Pr praseodymium	60 Nd neodymium	61 Pm promethium	62 Sm samarium	63 Eu europium	64 Gd gadolinium	65 Tb terbium	66 Dy dysprosium	67 Ho holmium	68 Er erbium	69 Tm thulium	70 Yb ytterbium	71 Lu lutetium
90 Th thorium	91 Pa protactinium	92 U uranium	93 Np neptunium	94 Pu plutonium	95 Am americium	96 Cm curium	97 Bk berkelium	98 Cf californium	99 Es einsteinium	100 Fm fermium	101 Md mendelevium	102 No nobelium	103 Lr lawrencium

Title:	Anotomical 3D KS3 Science uJ	
Client:	KJA	Font: Arial reg. 11/13pt
Date:	2 Dec 2013	Rev: 16 Dec 2013
		18 Dec 2013

THE SI SYSTEM

There is an international standard system of units of measurement, called the **SI system**. All the units in the SI system have defined values. So anyone who uses these units knows that everyone else will understand exactly what the measurement is. The table on the right shows many of these units.

You may find other units for some of these quantities (e.g. inches for length). In science, we always use SI units.

Quantity measured	Name of unit	Symbol
length	metre	m
mass	kilogram	kg
time	second	s
force	newton	N
area	square metres	m^2
volume	cubic metres	m^3
temperature	degrees Celsius	°C
speed	metres per second	m/s
current	ampere or amp	A
energy	joule	J
voltage	volt	V
pressure	pascal	Pa
power	watt	W
frequency	hertz	Hz

Standard prefixes

Sometimes the SI units are not a convenient size, so we use bigger or smaller versions. For instance, it is a bit awkward to measure the thickness of a leaf in metres! It is much easier to use millimetres. An extra part is added to the name of the unit and to its symbol to show we are using a bigger or smaller version. These additions are called **prefixes**.

Prefix	Symbol	Meaning	Example
mega-	M	1 000 000	1 megawatt (1 MW) = 1000 000 W
kilo-	k	1000	1 kilojoule (kJ) = 1000 J
deci-	d	1/10	1 cubic decimetre (dm^3) = 1/1000 m^3 (1/10 m × 1/10 m × 1/10 m)
centi-	c	1/100 (a hundredth)	100 centimetres (cm) = 1 m
milli-	m	1/1000 (a thousandth)	1000 millimetres (mm) = 1 m
micro-	μ	1/1 000 000 (a millionth)	1000 micrometres (μm) = 1 mm
nano-	n	1/1 000 000 000	1 000 000 nanometres (nm) = 1 mm

Other units

There are some units that are still commonly used, which do not fit the standard pattern.

Quantity	Standard unit	Other units still used
time	seconds	minutes, hours, days, years
length	metres	miles
speed	m/s	kilometres per hour (km/h), miles per hour (mph)
volume	m^3	litres (1 litre = 1000 cm^3 = 1 dm^3), millilitres (1 ml = 1 cm^3)

HAZARD SYMBOLS

Many things around a lab have special signs on them warning you of danger. The signs in diamonds below are internationally agreed symbols that you might find on chemicals:

	This symbol warns that a chemical may harm your health if you do not use it properly. The word 'irritant' might be found near this symbol and means that the chemical may give you a rash if you get it on you or make you choke if you breathe it in.

	This symbol tells you that a chemical is corrosive. It will attack your skin if you get it on you.		This symbol tells you that a chemical can cause a serious health problem if you breathe it in (e.g. an allergic reaction, an asthma attack, breathing difficulties).
	This symbol warns you that a chemical is flammable. It catches fire easily.		This symbol warns you that a chemical is oxidising. This means that it can provide a source of oxygen for a fire and make the fire worse.
	This symbol means that a chemical is poisonous (toxic). Poisons can kill.		This symbol warns you that a chemical is very poisonous to water organisms. Chemicals like this should not be released into the environment.

You may also see warning signs like this:

	This is a general warning sign. It may be placed in an area where there is some broken glass or a spilt chemical. Or it may just remind you to be particularly careful when doing something or using particular pieces of equipment or chemicals.

	This symbol means that there is a risk of getting an electric shock.		This 'biohazard' symbol means that there is a certain living thing in an area that may make you ill.

Some symbols tell you to do things so that you stay safe:

	This symbol reminds you to wear safety glasses or goggles when working in a certain area or using particular pieces of equipment or chemicals.		This symbol reminds you to wash your hands after you have done an experiment.

Published by Pearson Education Limited, 80 Strand, London, WC2R 0RL.

www.pearsonschools.co.uk

Text © Pearson Education Limited 2019
Writers: Mark Levesley, Sue Kearsey, Ian Bradley, Alice Jenson, Sarah Longshaw, Penny Johnson
Series editor: Mark Levesley
Edited by Just Content
Typeset by PDQ Digital Media Solutions Ltd.
Original illustrations © Pearson Education Limited 2019
Cover photo © Shutterstock.com: Kletr

The rights of Mark Levesley, Sue Kearsey, Ian Bradley, Alice Jenson, Sarah Longshaw, Penny Johnson to be
identified as authors of this work have been asserted by them in accordance with the Copyright, Designs
and Patents Act 1988.

First published 2019

24
17

British Library Cataloguing in Publication Data
A catalogue record for this book is available from the British Library

ISBN 978 1292 29410 0

Printed in Great Britain by Bell and Bain Ltd, Glasgow

Note from the publisher
Pearson has robust editorial processes, including answer and fact checks, to ensure the accuracy of the
content in this publication, and every effort is made to ensure this publication is free of errors. We are,
however, only human, and occasionally errors do occur. Pearson is not liable for any misunderstand-
ings that arise as a result of errors in this publication, but it is our priority to ensure that the content is
accurate. If you spot an error, please do contact us at resourcescorrections@pearson.com so we can make
sure it is corrected.